Max Weber and the Methodology
of the Social Sciences

Max Weber and the Methodology of the Social Sciences

Toby E. Huff

Transaction Books
New Brunswick (U.S.A.) and London (U.K.)

Library of Congress Catalog Number: 83-9145

ISBN: 0-87855-945-0 (paper)

Printed in the United States of America

Library of Congress Cataloging in Publication Data

Huff, Toby E., 1942-
    Max Weber and the methodology of the social sciences.

    Includes index.
    1. Weber, Max, 1864-1920.   2. Social sciences—Methodology.
I. Title.
H59.W4H83   1983   300'.1   83-9145
ISBN 0-87855-945-0 (pbk.)

To the memory of
Benjamin Nelson (1911-77)
Scholar, teacher, and friend,
who took the path less traveled by

and

Talcott Parsons (1902-79)
Intrepid theorist and generous colleague

CONTENTS

PREFACE

The following volume is the lucky result of having run across a translation of Weber's *Roscher and Knies* while writing a more general study of the logic of sociological inquiry. That study was entitled *Discovery and Explanation: An Essay in the Logic and Method of Sociology*. But before that study reached completion, the present essay grew out of it.

My attention was drawn to the hermeneutic tradition in the social sciences by Robert Bellah's seminar "Tradition and Interpretation," sponsored by the National Endownment for the Humanities at the University of California at Berkeley (1976–77; Grant #F76-240). A year after that seminar I was a member of the Institute for Advanced Study in Princeton, New Jersey, where the main portion of the present study was written.

Although American readers of this volume may think that I have referred to a significant portion of the German literature on Weber, there is in fact a much larger body of material to which I have intentionally not referred due to limits of space and other considerations. Nevertheless, I am aware of the writings of such scholars as Horst Baier, Winfred Brugger, Karl-Otto Apel, Deiter Heinrich, Johannes Weiss, R. Prewo, R. Münch, and a number of others. And while one can learn much from them, on balance they are not generally attuned to the significance of what I have called the lessons of "the new materials in the philosophy and history of science." Moreover, none of these writers perceived the depth of the theoretical gulf which separated Weber from Dilthey and the phenomenological tradition.

There are a number of additional methodological questions central to Weber's enterprise about which I have said nothing. This too stems from the fact that the present volume is part of a larger study, and in the future I hope to fill in these omissions. For the present I should be content if this study contributed something to the effort to rethink the logic of explanation in the social sciences.

Chapter 1 of this volume appeared in the *Philosophy of the Social Sciences,* vol. 11 (1981), and chapters 2-3 in vol. 12 (1982).

INTRODUCTION

During the last two decades Western philosophical thought about the foundations of science has undergone a profound sea-change which has since come to be called "postempiricist philosophy of science." The familiar names associated with this revolution in the philosophy and history of science are those of N.R. Hanson, Karl Popper, Thomas Kuhn, P.K. Feyerabend, and Imré Lakatos, to name only the most influential. Between 1958 and 1970 this group of philosophers produced an extraordinary set of writings which radically altered the "orthodox" and positivist account of science (cf. Suppe 1974).[1]

Most simply put, the result of these publications and the debate they engendered was a severe attack on the philosophical foundations of logical positivism, especially its unworkable distinction between "theoretical" and "observational" terms in the language of science (cf. Suppe 1974:66ff.). Furthermore, Karl Popper's attack on the widely held view that scientific progress rests on some clearly defined logical operations called "induction," coupled with N.R. Hanson's explorations in the "logic of discovery," and Kuhn's in the history of science, served to show that the process of scientific discovery—the process of conceptual innovation—is far more unpredictable, spontaneous, and discontinuous than the image of science fostered by the logical positivists would lead one to believe (cf. Popper 1959, 1968; Hanson 1958, 1961; Kuhn 1962). But while Popper and Hanson both suggested that scientific innovation is the product of "conjectures" or "retroductive inference" (to use Hanson's [1958, ch. 4] term borrowed from Peirce), Hanson rejected Popper's strictly hypothetico-deductive model of science, insisting instead that science has much more to discover than "covering laws." In the last essay he sent off for publication before his untimely death, Hanson sketched out "an anatomy of discovery" which made it clear that science seeks to discover not just laws but those entities, processes, mechanisms, and effects which constitute the fine structure of scientific explanation (see Hanson 1967).

The implications and ramifications of this philosophical movement are still being felt (and realized) in those disciplines outside of the philosophy of science. This revolution in the philosophy and history of science of the 1960s and 1970s has created a situation in which all previous accounts of scientific methodology and all histories of science are suspect (see Agassi 1963; Lakatos 1976). This caveat applies to sociology and all related social sciences whose practitioners have labored over works on the methodological foundations of their respective disciplines.

In such a context it is natural to ask—how would Max Weber's methodological writings fare if they were studied from the point of view of the lessons of the new materials in the philosophy and history of science? At first blush one might be inclined to think that Weber would fare badly, to think as W.G. Runciman apparently does, that Weber's "view of natural science . . . was a rather restricted one by twentieth-century standards" (1972:68). Even the most sympathetic defenders of Weber's enterprise centered on the nature and implications of the Protestant ethic thesis are disposed to dodge the question, preferring to say: "Whether or not Weber's theory of concept formation in the social sciences is sound is, of course, a moot point" (Marshall 1982:51).

But here we should be more attentive to the details of Weber's extraordinary methodological discussions—especially his early methodological essays of 1903-07—and to the fact that logical positivism was a philosophical movement which emerged on the historical scene after Weber's death. Of course, one can trace the historical roots of positivism back to Comte and Mill (and even earlier; see Kolakowski 1969; Popkin 1964; Lenzer 1975). But the positivism of which contemporary social scientists (and many philosophers of science) despair is the logical positivism of the Vienna Circle (cf.Kraft 1953; Passmore, 1967; Feigl 1969). And while some of the positivists traced their spiritual origins to Ernst Mach, it should be noted that (1) Weber had read Mach's writings and was by no means a convert to them, and (2) the use of Mach's work to justify the program of the logical positivists has been emphatically challenged by contemporary philosophers of science, above all P.K. Feyerabend (1980). Similarly, the "covering law" model can be traced back to John Stuart Mill, and Weber's dislike of it turns up in numerous places.

If we are to make any sense out of the confusing and multifarious debates regarding the methodology of the social sciences, and above all, progress in understanding Weber's own methodological position, we must first review the history of logical positivism and the recent critique of it advanced by the postempiricist philosophers of science. Without that grounding we are prone to judge the issues (and Weber's discussions of them) in an anachronistic fashion. A great deal of the recent criticism of Weber (of the late 1950s to the present) stems from a failure of Weber's critics *and* supporters to develop a philosophically informed account of the *natural* sciences, one rooted in the new materials in the philosophy and history of science. Without an immersion in those materials, and without a better image of science than that supplied by logical positivism, the chances of successful resolution of the fundamental issues remain remote.[2]

For present purposes we need only a brief sketch of the rise and fall of logical positivism to get our bearings regarding the issues at hand. Once we have covered that terrain, we can more easily approach the various questions regarding interpretation and understanding, and the role of laws and causal inference in the social sciences.

THE RISE AND FALL OF LOGICAL POSITIVISM

Until the appearance of the new materials in the philosophy and history of science, philosophers of science gave almost exclusive attention to the problem of formulating rules of *logic* for casting scientific theories—once gotten—into formal deductive chains of inference. The move by the logical positivists during the first third of the century to abandon the search for rules of induction was a move toward deductionism, and it also produced a distorted image of the scientific enterprise. Among social scientists, this deductionist image of "good scientific theory" is very strong in certain quarters, particularly among the theory constructionists. George Homans (1961, 1964, 1967) has been the most insistent exponent of this view that theories *must* be deductive formalisms (and cf. Zetterberg 1955, 1965).

To appreciate how this state of affairs came about and how this view gained such prominence among philosophers of science *prior* to the *new materials,* we must look at the history of the consolidation of the positivist movement into "logical positivism." The general contours of this development are well known (Kraft 1953; Feigl 1969; Passmore 1967; von Mieses 1951), and its inspiration may be partly traced to the *historical* studies of science by Ernst Mach. Mach's studies in the history of the science of mechanics alerted some philosophers of science to the fact that more than a few ideas in the history of scientific discourse could not be logically or empirically justified. One might even say that they were metaphysical: they transcend empirical proof or confirmation (Mach 1960).

The brilliant innovations of Einstein in 1905 and thereafter (who in fact considered himself a follower of Mach's "philosophy") produced theories in sharp contrast to the prevailing scientific attitudes. The results of the eclipse observations of 1919 confirmed the predictions drawn from Einstein's new theory of gravitation and thereby brought back the corpuscular theory of light which had been (so it was thought) decisively refuted by the experiments of Young and Fresnal in the early nineteenth century (cf. Hanson 1963:9ff.). As a result of these developments, the house of science seemed to be in disorder. In the words of the physicist P.W. Bridgman, "it was a great shock to discover [after Einstein's work] that classical concepts, accepted unquestionably, were inadequate to meet the actual situation" (1953 [1928]:34).

This conceptual chaos stimulated a variety of philosophers and mathematically trained individuals, especially a group called the Vienna Circle, to do something about it. Their collective endeavors spawned several groups, including one called The Ernst Mach Society (Kraft 1953:5), and most important of all, the philosophical movement known as "logical positivism."

With the collapse of conclusive faith in the intellectual structure of classical mechanics brought on by the rise of quantum mechanics, there was a corresponding quandary regarding the ontological status of the *concepts* of science. The Kantian rejection of knowledge of "the thing-in-itself," a conception which Mach (1914:6) regarded as a "monstrous" idea, led increasingly to instrumentalism (sometimes called "fictionalism") and conventionalism in philosophy of science. According to these philosophical views, scientific theories (and laws) are either "calculating devices" (which critics have noted, "work where they work"), or simply conventions which serve as useful descriptions of nature but are not thought to be "real" descriptions of nature or the natural world. As Karl Popper pointed out, the path to this stance can be traced back at least to Bishop Berkeley in the seventeenth century. Berkeley railed against "meaningless" terms, hidden or "occult" forces, belief in the real "essence" of things, and suggested instead that the true task of natural philosophers ("mechanical philosophers") was the discovery of laws of nature and not causes (see Popper 1968, ch.6; Mill 1969: 266ff.). In brief, the "crisis of the European sciences" at the turn of the century regarding the status of our knowledge about the world ushered in strongly instrumentalist and conventionalist views of scientific knowledge.

While the logical positivists were reluctant to adopt a realist view of science (cf. Feyerabend 1964), they wanted above all to remove metaphysics from science. In an effort to carry out this mission, they introduced a variety of logical devices and rules of proper language use. For them, reforming science was reforming the *language* of science.

Predictably, these efforts shifted from the attempt to eliminate "meaningless" terms through the use of methods of "verification," to the principle of testability and then to *operationalism* (see Bridgman 1953). Karl Popper's criticism of the Vienna Circle's effort to eliminate "meaningless" words resulted in his formulation of the notion of falsifiability, which also underwent change (see Popper 1968, ch.11; Lakatos 1970). Popper's criterion shifted attention from the elimination of metaphysics to the problem of demarcating science from pseudoscience.

In the minds of the logical positivists, the effort to eliminate meaningless terms in science was linked to the project of providing a revision of the language of science (Kraft 1953:5), and it was in this sense that science was to be reconstructed. But the more radical element of this position was its deliberate effort to eliminate anything—any term—that went beyond immediate experience, that is, to eliminate unobservables which might be thought to be metaphysical entities. In seeking to rid science of such notions as "absolute time" and "absolute space," as well as "force," Ernst Mach significantly contributed to the evolution of Einstein's relativity theory. But conversely, Mach's antiatomism had the effect of driving a wedge between the two men as well as between Mach and the emerging microparticle physicists, who were beginning to advance a very sophisticated theory of unobservables (see Holton 1973, ch.8; Hiebert 1970; Blackmore 1972).

The thrust of the logical positivists' reconstruction was geared to substitute symbolic logic and a new mathematical notation for the "ordinary language" of science. Because the logical positivists centered their attention exclusively on the logical form of scientific theories, the view began to emerge that the analysis of science was a purely formal examination of the relations between terms and propositions. Matters of fact and their connections to scientific theories became secondary and were given back to the special sciences:

With the help of symbolism [it was said] a form of representation has been found which enables mathematically precise formulation of concepts and propositions and rules governing the latter's combination. Thus it becomes possible to operate in a purely formal manner without regard to context, a sort of calculus of conceptions and propositions [Kraft 1953:18].

By this reasoning, the logic of science was completely divorced from substantive and empirical questions:

The logic of science is not concerned with *empirical* analysis of these concepts, which is the task of the special sciences, but only with *logical* analysis. Whatever is a question of fact must be answered by . . . one of the special sciences, and is thus no philosophical question. The latter kind of question can concern only the logical structure of scientific knowledge [Kraft 1953:25-26].

The substitution of symbolic logic as *the* tool of logical analysis served to remove philosophy of science—or "logic of science" as it was then known—from questions about how one arrives at scientific assertions in the first place. The context of discovery was thereby severed from the logic of science. A rigid distinction between the context of discovery and that of justification, or proof, became the order of the day. Whereas F.C.S. Schiller (1917:260) had drawn the distinction to urge the exploration of what the role of logic ought to be in scientific inference, others, such as Hans Reichenbach (1938:7-8), drew the distinction only to render the study of the history and logic of discovery irrelevant.

It was a *point d'honneur* on the part of the logical positivists to avoid the study of the history of science (a matter of facts) and consequently of how any particular scientific theory came into existence. The arguments that scientists used to establish their theories were severed from the logic of science. Perhaps this was what Mach intended, but it remained for the postempiricist philosophers of science, especially Hanson, Kuhn, and Feyerabend in the late twentieth century to bring the *history* of science back into focus in order to illuminate the *philosophy* of science. To a degree, this was true of Popper also.

However, the assumption that matters of fact are purely empirical questions (of no importance to philosophy of science) rests on the suppressed assumption that facts and theory are unrelated epistemologically, that it is possible to construct a pure observation language. Such a view is now regarded (as it was by Whewell in the early nineteenth century and by Peirce in the late nineteenth century) as naive. This intellectual slight of hand was made to work by the logical positivists—at least until the appearance of the postempiricist philosophers of science.

The realization that science historically has followed a zig-zag course littered with "illogical" notions triggered a reaction designed to blot out this unconscionable development. In Bridgman's (1953:34) view:

We should now make it our business to understand so thoroughly the character of our permanent mental relations to nature that another change in our attitude, such as that due to Einstein, shall be forever impossible. It was perhaps excusable that a revolution in mental attitude should occur once, because after all physics is a young science, and physicists have been very busy, but it would certainly be a reproach if such a revolution should ever prove necessary again.

With such an inspiration the logical positivists formulated an ideal image of science alleged to be consistent with a philosophy of empiricism, with the additional virtue of being a logically unified set of propositions (see Feyerabend 1965a), although after Gödel's work, no system—no purely formal system (see Davis 1965)—could claim to be logically complete. Nevertheless, this reconstructed science was to be built up from a finite set of "primitive terms," "protocol sentences," and the like, into a completely unified set of axioms, postulates, and propositions. But if science were to be remade according to these assumptions, then it would become a problem to determine how these scientific assertions were attached to the empirical world. According to Feigl's (1969:16-17) depiction of this enterprise (thought up by Schlick),

the entire deductive system, that is, the postulates (implicit definitions), together with explicit definitions of equally uninterpreted, purely formal concepts (as well as all derivable theorems), form a "free-floating" structure. If this structure is to be given empirical significance, it must be anchored by "coordinate definitions" (Reichenbach's term) or "correspondence rules" (Carnap's term) to some data on the level of observation.

In terms of scientific practice, this is "backwards science." Science generally *begins* with puzzling, problematic empirical evidence (or in Popper's words, a problem), and then sets about trying to invent concepts and theories which will explain it. But the logical positivists, since they were attempting to reconstruct an existing set of confused and imprecise assertions, could begin at the other end, with purely formal sets of primitives, axioms, postulates, and the like. Confusion about this starting point arises only if one forgets that the positivist program was a reconstruction of science, not a set of rules for doing science.

It could be said that Carnap and others, including Carl Hempel in the 1950s, were not clear about what they were doing. The appearance of books (part of the *International Encyclopedia of Unified Science*) bearing such titles as *The Technique of Theory Construction* (Woodger 1970 [1939]) and *Fundamentals of Concept Formation in Empirical Science* (Hempel 1972 [1939]), encouraged their readers to believe that they purported to tell them how empirical sciences operate. Subsequently, this image of science, complete with primitive terms, axioms, postulates, and rules of reduction (as well as rules of correspondence) was imported by sociological theory constructionists. Prime illustrations are found in Zetterberg's "On Axiomatic Theories in Sociology" (1955, 1965); *Sociological Theory Construction* (Gibbs 1972); Mullins's "Theory Construction from Available Materials" (1974); and Hage's *Techniques of Theory Construction in Sociology* (1972), among others. The difference between these manuals of instruction and those of the logical positivists is that the former unabashedly claim to provide rules of instruction that will yield important scientific theories, whereas the logical positivists wanted only to correct or reconstruct the scientific theories which had already been invented.

By the mid-sixties, the logical positivists began to realize what had happened and became more cautious in stating the goals of their enterprise. Hempel (1965:6) pointed out that

the quest for rules of induction in the original sense of the canons of scientific discovery has to be replaced, in the logic of science, by the quest for general objective criteria determining (A) whether, and—if possible—even (B) to what degree, a hypothesis H may be said to be corroborated by a given body of evidence E. This approach differs essentially from the inductivist conception of the problem in that it *presupposes* not only E, but also H as given, and then seeks to determine a certain logical relationship between them.

The logical positivists' apparent rules of theory construction are rules of *reconstruction*: one must first have a theory, or a hypothesis, along with the evidence on which it is based. Then one can proceed to determine if a particular set of formal conceptions is internally consistent and if the formally stated theory is corroborated by existing evidence. But *what is left out is the process by which a theory is found in the first place.* Trivial theories are presumably commonplace, and the logical positivists were not claiming that they could supply rules or techniques which would allow anyone to discover new theories. That is, they did not think that they were supplying rules which would allow anyone to become a Galileo, a Newton, a Maxwell, Planck, Bohr, or Einstein. They were not aiming at the construction of a logic machine. Nevertheless, if the works on theory construction is sociology are any measures of this, sociological theory constructionists have unwittingly misunderstood the intent of the logical positivists.

In any event, after the appearance of the new materials in the philosophy and history of science, *après le déluge,* some of the remaining logical positivists were willing to concede that their modes of procedure were highly artificial accounts of scientific practice. As Herbert Feigl (1970:13) put it, "it should be stressed and not merely bashfully admitted, that the rational reconstruction of theories is a highly artificial hindsight operation which has little to do with the work of the creative scientist." But unfortunately, the damage had been done, and social scientists continue to operate with this artificial image of science-in-the-making.

Before leaving this topic of deductive theory building, we ought to make clear an additional element of the alleged virtues of deductivism. According to the early logical positivists (and contemporary sociological theory constructionists), if one begins with unequivocal terms, definitions, rules of transformation, and the like, it ought to be possible to build a giant theoretical edifice "of skyscrapper dimensions" (Merton 1969:71). The assumptions here are two: (1) that it *is* possible to fix "the protocol sentences," the most basic terms of a science at the *outset,* and (2) that having done that, all additional empirical content can be simply added on, cumulated, as it were, in a straightforward manner (cf. Merton 1968:71ff.; Mullins 1974).

The problems with this view are legion. First, how is it possible to set out with all the conceptually important terms of a science, *before* it has done its year (centuries?) of research? If the concepts and associated abstract terms of a science are invented to organize "the chaotic diversity of our sense experience" (Einstein), then the concepts must come *after* the multitude of sensory experience. And how are we to know that no additional, new, and possibly anomalous experiences are going to occur? On the other hand, as Kuhn, Feyerabend, and others have noted, no theory ever fit all the facts, and we are always faced with the possibility that a better set of concepts is near at hand which will more accurately "fit the data" (Kuhn 1962:40, 146; Feyerabend 1965a:224).

Second, if by chance two researchers—each with equally precise terms, definitions, etc.—set out with incommensurable theories—how are these two logically incompatible theories to be reduced to a common set of terms? Surely not by deduction (cf. Maull 1977). The corpuscular and wave theories of light are illustrations of this dilemma, and over the centuries one or the other theory triumphed, only to be set aside again at a later date. Likewise, there was a logical (mathematical) disjunction between the laws of motion worked out by Kepler (his cube root law) and Newton (the inverse square law). In whatever fashion Newton arrived at the famous inverse square law of gravity, it could not be "deduced" or "logically derived" from Kepler's cube root law (see Cohen 1974a,b; Hanson 1961:31-34; Popper 1972:197ff; Wilson 1974).

Third, from an inferential point of view, science begins with facts, data, and anomalous bits of evidence. By what set of operations are we to arrive at the major premise, that from which all the evidence at hand can be deduced? It is obvious that this cannot be done by deduction, and that there are *no rules* for making valid inferences of this sort. The deductionist account of science is most seriously lacking when it comes to saying something about the process by which scientists arrive at their theoretical conceptions. Any informed view of the *practice* of science ought to begin with a realization that science-in-the-making is a process of theory finding, or making guesses and conjectures, not of restating and testing hypotheses already gotten.[3]

Close students of Thomas Kuhn's work will not have forgotten that if there is anything to the notion of paradigms and paradigm shifts, it is clear that when paradigms do shift, "what were ducks in the scientist's world before the revolution are rabbits afterward" (Kuhn 1962:110). Moreover, the appearance of a

new theory implies a change in the rules governing the prior practice of normal science. Inevitably . . . it reflects upon much scientific work . . . already successfully completed. That is why a new theory, however special its range of application, is seldom or never just an increment to what is already known. Its assimilation requires the reconstruction of prior theory and the re-evaluation of prior fact, an intrinsically revolutionary process that is seldom completed by a single man and never overnight [Kuh. 1962:7].

Even if this be an overstatement, it is sufficiently clear that incommensurable theories do exist in abundance in the social sciences (as in the natural sciences), and finding ways to reconcile them is more than a problem of working out primitive terms, axioms, postulates, and rules of correspondence. In short, Hanson argued, by the time someone starts to create a hypothetico-deductive chain of inference by reformulating a less tightly knit network of inference, really creative thinking is over (Hanson 1958:70).

WEBER AND POSITIVISM

Given this brief sketch of the rise and fall of logical positivism and the new image of science which emerged from the critique of logical positivism by the postempiricist philosophers of science, we may momentarily return to Weber's case. Virtually all the criticism leveled by postempiricist philosophers of science against logical positivism can be found in Weber's early methodological writings (those published during 1903-07). Although some writers are inclined to disparage Weber's deep philosophical grounding in neo-Kantian philosophy, this is the primary philosophical capital—combined with Weber's brilliance in applying it—which makes his writings so presciently contemporary.

Weber was a keen student of the writings of the philosophers and logicians of science of his day. In the first instance, he was an avid reader of Rickert's *The Limits of Concept Formation in the Natural Sciences* (1902), and found what Rickert wrote there to be "*very* good." In contrast to the (later) logical positivist search for secure foundations (also sought by Husserl and his followers), both Weber and Rickert insisted that there could be no definitive, logically closed system of scientific theory, even in the natural sciences. For Rickert and Weber, the world was an infinite, "inexhaustible manifold" of possibilities, and every attempt to provide a definitive description of some domain was only a more or less arbitrary conceptual starting point. As Rickert (1962 [1898]:32) put it:

One need only make an attempt to "describe" reality *exactly* "as it is," i.e., to achieve a conceptual representation of it faithful in all its details, to realize very soon how futile such an undertaking is. Empirical reality proves to be an *immeasurable manifold* which seems to become greater and greater the more deeply we delve into it and begin to analyze it. . . . For even the "smallest" part contains more than any mortal man has the power to describe. Indeed, the part of reality that man can include in his concepts, and thus in his knowledge, is almost infinitesimally small when compared to what he must disregard.

In the words of a distinguished contemporary philosopher of science, science is an "unended quest" (cf. Popper 1976:130ff.). In this context, no one will overlook the fact that Popper's philosophy of science, and thus that of his many followers (past and present), is affected by a neo-Kantian influence (see Popper, 1968, ch.8; Lieberson, 1982a,b).

In addition to being a serious student of Rickert's writings (which bear an interesting and favorable comparison with Popper's), Weber was widely read in the works of Hermann von Helmholtz, the preeminent scientist of the nineteenth century, as well as those of Mach, Wundt, Husserl, the physiologist von Kries, and numerous others, not to mention the names of the many historians and related social scientists whose work he read. The importance of Weber's wide reading in the literature of the natural sciences (of his day) will become evident as the reader progresses in the study which follows.

It is anachronistic at best to ascribe to Weber a commitment to positivism insofar as the latter was the product of the Vienna Circle. Nevertheless, students of Weber with backgrounds as diverse as those of Friedrich Tenbruck, Peter Winch, and W.G. Runciman (among others), have attributed assorted "positivist moorings" and elements of "naturalistic positivism" (Tenbruck 1959:598) to Weber. Winch's (1958) charge is rather amorphous, but his general critique rests on his belief that Weber was too sympathetic to "the natural science model." I shall leave further discussion of Winch's views for the concluding section of chapter 3, and readers of the following pages can judge for themselves where Weber stood.

The critique of Weber's philosophy of science by W.G. Runciman is so curious and elliptical that it may be well to add a few remarks. According to Runciman (1972:15), "Weber was wrong on three issues: the difference between theoretical presuppositions and implicit value judgements; the manner in which 'ideographic' explanations are to be subsumed under causal laws; and the relation of explanation to description."

The role of value judgements in Weber's work is very complex and the limits of the present introduction prevent further discussion of it. H.H. Bruun's excellent study, *Science, Values, and Politics in Max Weber's Methodology* (1972), should serve to demonstrate both the origins and consistency of Weber's position on this matter. On the other hand, the claim that Weber was mistaken regarding the presumed subsumption of "ideographic" explanations (of historical and sociological data) under causal laws rests on a series of misconceptions, several of which are set out (without any reference to the present context) at the conclusion of the study (see pp. 67-73 below).

I have suggested above that Weber can hardly be called a positivist since the whole logical positivist movement erupted after his death, and that insofar as the early roots of positivism are concerned, Weber was not unaware of them. However, if one wishes to define commitment to the nomological (hypothetico-deductive) model as the critical element in a positivist identity, one discovers that this element is the one Weber most emphatically rejected, and for a variety of very good reasons which issue from both an analysis of the role of laws in the natural sciences and from the point of view of the sciences of man. It is here that Runciman's critique of Weber is so curious, for he claims "that it would be even more inaccurate to classify Weber an Idealist rather than a Positivist" (1972:17), and that Weber was almost in "complete agreement with the Positivists," except that "he fights shy" of this (p. 69). Yet the one doctrine which would clearly identify Weber with the classical positivists (J.S. Mill and Karl Menger), namely the belief in the indispensability of causal laws as the foundation stone for social scientific explanation, is the one doctrine that Weber most consistently rejected: "Weber's denial of the applicability of general laws in the social sciences," Runciman thinks (p. 61), is an error which needs correcting. It is even claimed that Weber's "view of 'cause' itself has now an undeniably old-fashioned air." As we shall see later, in the light of the writings of Hart and Honoré (1959), Donald Davidson (1968), and a variety of other contemporary philosophers of the social sciences, including Morton White, this claim itself is dated.[4]

In short, Runciman alleges that Weber was a positivist of sorts, yet the most basic element in such an identity, belief in the necessity of causal laws, is missing in Weber's methodology. All this leads to the conclusion that students and critics of Weber who have ascribed positivist leanings to him have done so on the basis of superficial readings of his methodological essays as well as a superficial understanding of what "positivism" might mean (cf. Giedymin 1975).

Although Weber was not a defender of the hypothetico-deductive model of science, he did insist that interpretive sociology attempts to arrive at causal explanations of social action. As he (1981:157) argued in the 1913 essay, "Some Categories of Interpretive Sociology," "Sociology must reject the assumption that 'understanding' [*Verstehen*] and causal 'explanation' have *no* relationship to one another." What Weber meant by "causal" explanation has often eluded students of Weber. None of the standard accounts of Weber's methodology, even Talcott Parsons's (1937) decidedly superlative discussions of it, are satisfactory (if even vaguely correct). It is obvious, *pace* Runciman (1972:61-68), that Weber rejected the possible use of the putative "laws of psychology" as linchpins in sociological explanation. Weber's reasons for this rejection of psychological laws will become evident as our inquiry proceeds.

For the present context, we need to stress only that given the fact that Weber subscribed neither to the nomological model nor the "laws of psychology" thesis, it is egregious to charge him with being any sort of positivist. The only possible grounds left for suggesting this idea would seem to be Weber's insistence on the fashioning of causal explanations in sociology and the social sciences generally. Granted Weber's rejection of the nomological model, the only context in which an objection to his commitment to causal explanation arises is that of interpretive or hermeneutic social science. There one finds the assertion that "the human studies" seek interpretations not explanations—explanations that would presumably be tainted by reference to implicit elements of the natural science model. It should not come as a surprise that this controversy goes back to Wilhelm Dilthey (1833-1911), although until now commentators on both Weber and Dilthey have failed to notice the former's sharp attacks of the latter, and more generally, of the descriptive psychology school.

To unravel this controversy and hope to do more than simply isolate a few issues, we must be prepared to probe deeper into the epistemological foundations of theory and observation, of interpretation and perception, than most participants in the debate have been willing to do. This is what Weber did, but until the recent translation of *Roscher and Knies,* no one seems to have noticed this and its consequences for the methodology of the social sciences. In the last two decades, under the influence of Gadamer (1975 [1960]) and Habermas (1971 [1968]), the view that the "human studies" are *uniquely* interpretive has gained considerable ground in certain quarters. The most sophisticated defense of it is found in Charles Taylor's "Interpretation and the Science of Man" (1971).[5] But to evaluate the claims of the new hermeneutics we need to consider the epistemological foundations of interpretation against the background of the critique of "objectivism" as it has been called by the hermeneuts (see Habermas 1971: esp. 69, 89, 307ff.; Ricoeur 1974:8), which is to be found in the new materials of postempiricist philosophy of science. This is nothing other than the problem of the theory-laden character of observation. We shall leave further discussion of Weber's conception of causal explanation for later.

OBSERVATION AND INTERPRETATION

According to Charles Taylor, "any science which can be called 'hermeneutic,' even in an extended sense, must be dealing with" some form of meaning (1971:3). Hence it must be a study of some "field of objects" in which it is possible to distinguish between "the sense or coherence" found in some object of study and the more fragmentary expression of that meaning in some concrete fragments of evidence. And since this enterprise concerns the science of man, this sense and coherence should somehow be "connected to a 'subject.' " This stress on the importance of (presumably) human subjects seems to me essential, but on the other hand, not all text analogues which have been construed to be meaningful by human subjects have been authored by men. The medievals took the starry heavens to be a book of nature, and this metaphor was of decisive importance in the rise of modern science (see Nelson 1981, ch.9). The important question is: what are the criteria of judgment in a hermeneutic science? According to Taylor (1971:5),

a successful interpretation is one which makes clear the meaning originally present [in a text or text analogue] in a confused, fragmentary, cloudy form. But how does one know that this interpretation is correct? Presumably because it makes sense of the original text: what is strange, mystifying, puzzling, contradictory is no longer so, is accounted for.

This hermeneutic view of the sciences of man suggests that we study and investigate various human expressions embodied in texts, text analogues, artifacts, and the like, because these expressions are frequently strange, puzzling, or anomalous —they are in "some way . . . confused, incomplete, cloudy, seemingly contradictory" (p.3). Accordingly, we resort to some form of interpretive activity.

The outcome of this interpretative effort must always be uncertain—or hypothetical—because "such uncertainty is an ineradicable part of our epistemological predicament" (p.6). Escape from this condition of tentativeness, Taylor (1971:7) argues, takes two forms, rationalist and empiricist. In the former, one simply arrives at "an understanding of such clarity that it would carry with it the certainty of the undeniable" (p.7). But it is the empiricist escape from subjectivity that is of interest to us, because here it is said that

the attempt is to reconstruct knowledge in such a way that there is no need to make final appeal to readings or judgments which can be checked further. That is why the basic building block of knowledge on this view is the impression, or sense-datum, a unit of information which is not the deliverance of a judgment, which has by definition no element in it of reading or interpretation, which is a brute datum.

This description of research activity is apparently meant to be a very abstract characterization of scientific research based on the supposed natural science model. What is striking about it is that it is a description of the building-block model of the logical positivists, and thus contains an implicit belief in such a model, appearing now some years after the postempiricist philosophers of science —Hanson, Popper, Kuhn, Feyerabend—had destroyed the credibility of that model, and when even Hanson's most vociferous critic was declaiming: "I do *not* claim that observations in science are mere sensations, pure sense impressions, raw sense data, etc., which are devoid of conceptual elements" (Kordig 1973:562; who in this regard follows Scheffler 1967).

The issue is both epistemological and factual—factual, if one grants that what physiological psychologists since the time of Helmholtz have to tell us about perception is allowed to bear on the issues. The problem concerns interpretation, and we want to know whether there is some special sense of interpretation that applies in the social sciences which does not apply in the natural sciences.

In the social sciences and human studies the problem is to interpret, to render meaningful some set of humanly inspired bits of evidence. So let us transform the problem of interpreting these bits of evidence into the task of interpreting "certain marks on a piece of paper" (Weber 1977:103) called a "text." If we do that, we can see that at this so-called sense-data level both the social and the natural scientist are confronted with puzzling, anomalous, visual stimuli. It will not do to say that the social scientist is dealing with "second-order" interpretations, whereas the natural scientist is dealing with "first-order" phenomena. Consider Duhem's (cited in Hanson 1971:4) famous example:

Enter a laboratory; approach the table crowded with an assortment of apparatus, an electric cell, silk-covered copper wire, small cups of mercury, spools, a mirror mounted on an iron bar; the experimenter is inserting into small openings the metal ends of ebony-headed pins; the iron bar oscillates, and the mirror attached to it throws a luminous band upon a celluloid scale; the forward-backward motion of this spot enables the physicist to observe the minute oscillations of the iron bar. But ask him what he is doing. Will he answer "I am studying the oscillations of an iron bar which carries a mirror"? No, he will say that he is measuring the electrical resistance of the spools. If you are astonished, if you ask him what his words mean, what relation they have with the phenomenon he has been observing and which you have noted at the same time as he, he will answer that you should take a course in electricity.

What could reference to "first-order" evidence mean in this case? Certainly Duhem's physicist is not operating with the everyday understanding of the layman. Nowadays almost all such experiments would be carried out with the use of very sophisticated electronic devices such as amp-meters, oscilloscopes, and the like, frequently monitored by computers. And today's astronomers rarely put their eyes to the telescope (except for fun and teaching undergraduates). Instead they record all the incoming signals electronically using radio telescopes, computers, and other automated devices to pinpoint the area of the heavens to be observed. Is this first-order, second-order, or third-order data? Today's physicist would regard the data gathered by Duhem's physicist as primitive, frail, and uncertain. Yet *both* sets of data represent the *interpretive* outcome of particular theories put to work through the use of electronic equipment with its own limits and operating assumptions.

But let us return to simple cases of observation. As Hanson (1958:15) put it, "seeing" something, a tree, a cathode-ray tube, a piece of poetry, is more than a photochemical reaction: "Seeing is not only the having of a visual experience; it is the way in which the visual experience is had." This is another way of accenting the sense "in which seeing is a 'theory-laden' undertaking. Observation of x is shaped by prior knowledge of x" (p.19). This could be translated into the language of experimental psychology as follows: "If an observer is 'set' to perceive the names of animals, he perceives the nonsense syllables *sael* and *wharl* as *seal* and *whale*. If, however, he is set to perceive something to do with boats, he perceives them as *sail* and *wharf*" (Hanson 1969:165, reporting on the work of experimental psychologists).

Some might think that there should be a distinction drawn between a psychological set and the influence of a theory. But consider the history of astronomy and the discovery of the planet Uranus. Prior to its discovery, the precise location in the sky of Uranus "had been observed . . . no less than seventeen times by first-rate observers without exciting their attention to anything remarkable" (Turner, 1963:6). Thus, not being "set" to see this new planet, astronomers did not see it, even though they were looking at the very place in the heavens where it would have been. And when its discoverer, William Herschel, did first report its citing, he reported a *comet!* So one is inclined to think that Herschel's theoretical expectations did shape his observations, leading him to interpret what he saw as a comet and not a planet.

Let us take another case of interpretive evaluation of observational evidence from the history of science, one from elementary particle physics. Between 1926 and 1932 physicists were conducting experiments which involved cloud chambers and the bombarding of targets with microparticles. At this time, scientific theory made it clear that there were only *two* fundamental particles in the universe. Consequently it has been said that "prior to the night of 2 August 1932 [when the positron was 'discovered'] the fundamental building stones of the physical world had been universally supposed to be simply protons and negative-electrons. Out of these two primordial entities all of the 92 elements had been formed" [Millikan as cited by Hanson 1963:152].

But while watching their cloud chambers several physicists encountered strange particles "coming up from the floor," or "backward-falling" particles, particles moving in the "wrong" direction. Because these particle tracks resembled backward-falling electrons moving in the wrong direction, they were "always overlooked, undervalued, or explained away" (Hanson 1963:139). They were declared to be spurious results, "dirt effects." Nevertheless, a photograph of such tracks was published in a leading physics journal in 1927, but no one at the time suggested that this photograph provided evidence of the existence of a new kind of particle. The photograph gave evidence of the generation of a form of antimatter, namely the positron (a positively charged electron—which was a contradiction in terms), but in the absence of a theoretical justification for its existence, the evidence of the senses was explained away as bad laboratory technique, dirt effects, and the like. Clearly, seeing a backward-falling electron is not the same as seeing a positron, although as a photochemical state of the eye they would seem to be identical. Here again we can grasp the consequences of the fact that observation contains an element of interpretation, because this is the way our perceptual apparatus works.

Interpretation is built into everything we perceive: sticks and stones, clerks and accountants (what would one look like?), sunrise, sunset, a literary text, and so on. And here we can find an easy passage back to Weber and the philosophy of science of the early twentieth century. The major founder of the empirist school of the psychology of perception (see Pastore 1971) was one of Weber's philosophical mentors, Hermann von Helmholtz. As he put it: "The sensations [of perception] are signs to our consciousness, and it is the task of our intelligence to learn to understand their meaning" (Helmholtz cited by Hanson 1958:177, n.2). Thus the various "marks on a piece of paper" we assume contain some meaning in the context of some particular cultural setting (and language), and which can be deciphered only by thinking about the various situated factors (motives and intentions, etc.) of the actors in question who may have authored the text or read it.

Likewise, we *assume* that the puzzling (and sometimes not so puzzling) evidence of our senses has some meaning vis-à-vis the lawful or "ultimate" structure of the universe (a metaphysical assumption). Whether these physical traces imply such meaning depends upon our theories and whether we decide that these particular tracings, effects, or events are "dirt affects," or that they make sense because they have reference to the putative underlying structures of nature. Moreover, Helmholtz (1962:14) insisted, "we are not simply passive to the impressions that are urged on us, but we *observe,* that is, we adjust our organs in those conditions that enable us to distinguish the impressions most accurately." When the term *meaning* arises in this context, we ought to be alerted to the fact that sense impressions have to be identified, assimilated to past experience, or otherwise we have just a "sensation." This is why psychologists of perception have made the distinction between sensation and perception (see Murch 1976:2). To grasp, to perceive the meaning of some sensory event is to connect it up to some set of meaning structures (in the mind or brain). For example, individuals who have been congenitally blind and who later benefited from cataract operations are confused about what they see after the operation, and only slowly do they develop the ability to recognize and identify even objects with which they are intellectually familiar. One psychologist described these processes of learning to see as follows:

The processes of identification and naming common objects by vision alone are for some time after the operation slow, laborious, inaccurate, and uncertain, particularly with objects exposed in varying spatial positions. The shortest period of time necessary to perceive even a small number of objects correctly is a month from the time of operation [Vernon 1952:10ff.].

And in 1878 Helmholtz (in Kahl 1971:382) declared:

The fact that people blind from birth who afterward gain their sight by an operation cannot, before they have touched them, distinguish between such simple forms as a circle and a square by the use of their eyes has been confirmed even more fully in recent studies.

In short, in all acts of perception there appears to be a set of higher-level operations, which in layman's terms, serve to interpret the sensory data so that it has some meaning (which is not to say that we first see and then interpret: the interpretation is in the seeing, and that is presumably why the world appears to be so unproblematic for most of us most of the time).[6]

That Weber was deeply influenced both by neo-Kantian philosophy and by Helmholtz is not in doubt. Weber's writings from his early methodological essays to "Science as a Vocation" are scattered with references to Helmholtz. Although I have not come across references to Helmholtz's handbook and writings on the physiology of perception in Weber's writings, there are references to and discussions of Helmholtz's very powerful and difficult epistemological essays on the axioms of geometry (see below, pp. 64f). It is obvious from the footnotes of *The Rational and Social Foundations of Music* (Weber 1958b) that Helmholtz's treatise *On the Sensations of Tone* (1954 [1862]) was a major source for Weber. Beyond that, the epistemological view that observation is theory-laden, or "in Goethe's words 'theory' is involved in the 'fact' " (Weber 1949:173), is clearly enough stated. Since this phrase appears as an epigraph for one of Rickert's chapters in *Die Grenzen,* it reveals the strong commitment to this view by both Weber and Rickert.

From Weber's (1949:106) point of view,

if one perceives the implications of the fundamental ideas of modern epistemology which ultimately derive from Kant, namely that concepts are primarily instruments for the intellectual mastery of empirical data and can be only that, the fact that precise genetic concepts are necessarily ideal types will not cause him to desist from constructing them.

How does one go about shaping these concepts in a particular situation?

It involves first the production of—let us say it calmly—"imaginary constructs" by the disregarding of one or more of those elements of "reality" which are actually present, and by the mental construction of a course of events, which is altered through modification of one or more "conditions" [1949:173].

But we need not pursue these questions further here. Such citations are only meant to show that Weber was far more attentive to the epistemological roots of knowledge than has been granted, and this awareness puts him in the forefront of what is today called "postempiricist" philosophy of science (though he was not a metaphyscial realist in Karl Popper's sense). For these reasons he could not be satisfied with the suggestions of the hermeneutic beginnings of his age (nor ours), because the questions raised "can be answered only by a *theory of interpretation,* a theory which at this point is barely visible and has hardly been explored at all" (Weber 1975:151).

WEBER AND PHENOMENOLOGY

We cannot conclude this introduction without adding some comments about the rise of the phenomenological movement. Though we have several good accounts of the rise of this movement, which began in the nineteenth century (see Farber 1967; Spiegelberg 1971), many social scientists today proceed as if it were a new perspective of the second third of this century, and as if Weber had been unaware of it. This is a myth, one which Alfred Schutz probably contributed to unwittingly. Nevertheless, it is in his writings (Schutz 1967; 1964-71) that one finds the suggestion that Weber's methodology, impressively developed as it is, requires the services of Husserl and phenomenology to rescue and correct it.[7]

The philosophical movement of phenomenology began with Husserl's teacher, Franz Brentano, in the 1870s (see Farber 1967:11ff.; Spiegelberg 1971:27ff.). Accordingly, Brentano's project to develop a new descriptive psychology (or phenomenology) was announced in his *Psychology from an Empirical Standpoint* (1973 [1874]). This project was characterized by a severe empiricism, proclaiming the need to get back to the unadultered facts. Brentano's means for achieving this goal was found in what he called our remarkable ability to achieve "inner perception" of mental (psychic) phenomena, and this inner perception (*innere Wahrnahmung*) was said to be characterized by its being immediate, infallible, and self-evident (Brentano 1973:91): "When we say that mental phenomena are those which are apprehended by means of inner perception, we say that this perception is immediately self-evident." This development constituted an extraordinary reversal of the epistemological status of the human and social sciences because now it appeared that inner psychic life could be understood with immediate and infallible means, whereas the natural sciences were stuck with observing "outer" reality and formulating hypotheses.

This cognitive self-assurance was the hallmark of Brentano's project to construct a descriptive psychology, and it was taken up very quickly by Wilhem Dilthey (see below, p. 30). As a result, some students of the movement have suggested that Brentano's notion of immediate self-evidence was a "necessary . . . and almost sufficient condition for the birth of Phenomenology" (Ryle 1971, vol. 1:200).

Although Husserl began as a self-professed student of Brentano, he challenged the idea of the self-evidence of inner perception in his *Logical Investigations* (1970 [1900]), and this was noted by Weber (1975:261, n.60). But thereafter Husserl brought back through the back door the same thesis, now presented as a process of "intuiting essences" through the phenomenological *epoché* (see Husserl 1931 [1913]:85, 110ff., 154ff., 92ff.). Consequently, as Ryle (1971:219) puts it, Husserl "ennobled this branch of philosophical enquiry with the quaint title 'phenomenology'; he credited it with the propriety method which he calls 'essential' or 'exemplary intuition'; and he claimed for it an absolute logical priority over all other philosophical, scientific, or historical enquiries."

All this was known to Max Weber. Weber, Rickert, and Husserl served together on the editorial board of the international journal of philosophy *Logos*. There is significant evidence throughout this whole period that Weber and Rickert were committed to all the implications of neo-Kantian philosophy, while Husserl (and Dilthey) stood in sharp contrast, committed to the quest for complete certainty (see Kolakowski 1975). This commitment led Husserl to search for that illusive propriety method of knowing that yields certainties, and which along the way made for an inevitable epistemological gulf between the men. When Rickert first published the outline of his philosophy of science in 1894 (in an essay titled "Toward a Theory of Scientific Concept Formation"), Husserl rejected Rickert's starting point, above all the latter's stress on the "extensive and intensive infinity" of reality and hence the inevitable conceptual relativity of science (Husserl 1894; Farber 1967:96ff.).

Likewise, when Dilthey's efforts to found a descriptive psychology (see below) are seen as part of the phenomenological movement originating in Brentano's work (and Husserl's and Dilthey's mutual reinforcement as well as correspondence is well known [see Ermarth 1978]), it becomes very difficult not to see Rickert's *Die Grenzen* as an attack on the foundations of the descriptive psychology movement. Weber observed: "In fact, it is the basic theme of his book *The Limits of Concept Formation in the Natural Sciences*—a book which—on this particular point—can be conceived as an attack on Dilthey's position" (1975 [1904]:239ff., n.16).

Many years later, Rickert took up the general philosophical problem of "unmediated" cognitive knowledge (*das Unmittelbare* [see Rickert 1923-24]), and he clearly attributes much of the confusion surrounding this problem to Husserl (Rickert 1923-24:242 n.1). In the middle of this somewhat hostile reception of phenomenology as a new and rigorous (quasi-psychological) science, Weber's discussions in *Roscher and Knies* of all the ideas associated with "immediate experience," "pure experience," and "self-evidence" may likewise be read as an unremitting attack on the "phenomenological point of view" (see below, for Weber's conclusions).

Until we carry out more detailed studies of the exchanges between Weber, Rickert, and Husserl, we shall lack a definitive answer to this question, but it is very probable that the ultimate influence vis-à-vis phenomenology was in the opposite direction from what contemporary social scientists assume: given the unrelenting attacks of Rickert and Weber (among others) on phenomenology and descriptive psychology, Husserl was forced to retreat to a position in which phenomenology was severed from the empirical sciences and therefore explicitly declared to be a nonempirical "science." Between 1900 and 1913 Husserl shifted his position, first denying the self-evidence of inner perception, then reembracing it under the more sophisticated theory of "immanent ideation." In the process, "pure phenomenology" was reborn as "pure transcendental phenomenology" completely divorced from factual concerns. In his *Ideas: General Introduction to Pure Phenomenology* (1931 [1913]:44), Husserl went out of his way to make this clear: "As over against this psychological 'phenomenology,' *pure or transcendental phenomenology will be established not as a science of facts, but as a science of essential Being* (as 'eidetic' science); a science which aims exclusively at establishing 'knowledge of essences' [*Wesenserkenntnisse*] and *absolutely no 'facts.'*"

Weber (1949:72), by contrast, was "interested in an *empirical science* of concrete reality": "We wish to understand on the one hand the relationships and the cultural significance of individual events in their contemporary manifestations and on the other the causes of their being *so* and not *otherwise.*"

In the 1970s a number of British and American sociologists began to recognize that Husserl's phenomenology was not the same as sociology's phenomenology, (see Heap and Roth 1973), and that even Alfred Schutz's phenomenological sociology contained severe limits, was not well suited to advance the cause of sociology generally (see Best 1975, 1978; Gorman 1975; Perinbanayagam 1975), and retained insurmountable defects in the area of comparative and historical inquiries as well. Perhaps now we shall have a better appreciation of the reasons why Weber took another path.

WEBER'S METHODOLOGICAL ESSAYS

Until the recent translation of Weber's three essays, *Roscher and Knies: The Logical Problems of Historical Economics* (1975), as well as *Critique of Stammler* (1977), access by English-language readers to the full range of Weber's methodological thought was severely limited. As a result, many commentators on Weber's methodological writings concluded that they were "fragmented," "incomplete," and only of secondary importance (cf. Torrance 1974). In part this was inevitable since what we had was only the second and fifth installments of a sequence of seven methodological essays, all written sequentially (and thematically unified) over a period of about five years (on which more below).

It is puzzling that those students of Weber who had access to the original German frequently failed to pay any attention to the methodological essays, or simply undervalued them. Thus Reinhard Bendix's classic study, *Max Weber: An Intellectual Portrait* (1960) neither mentions nor discusses the range of Weber's methodological writings, which in their German form constitute just short of 600 pages (excluding the "Science as a Vocation" essay; see Weber 1922). Similarly, Tenbruck (1980) praises Bendix's neglect of Weber's methodological writings, disparages their study, and thereby appears to follow his earlier view that "as a whole, Max Weber's methodology has nothing of substantive importance to tell us" (1959:625).[8] We saw earlier in the case of W.G. Runciman that appreciation of Weber's methodological achievements is not quite what one would expect from close followers of Weber. Consequently, Talcott Parsons's study of

Weber's methodology (in chapter 16 of *The Structure of Social Action* [1937]) remains one of the most important. In considerable measure, Parsons's study was influenced by von Schelting's classic work, *Max Weber's Wissenschaftslehre* (1934), probably still the best study in that language.

The recent translations of *Roscher and Knies* and *Critique of Stammler* mark a new beginning in the understanding of Weber's methodological thought. But readers of those essays should be alerted to the fact that the essays in *Roscher and Knies* were written together—in a sequentially and thematically coherent fashion —with the two major essays, " 'Objectivity' in Social Science and Social Policy" (Weber 1949 [1904]:49-112), and "Critical Studies in the Logic of the Cultural Sciences" (1949 [1906]:113-88). Accordingly, the first essay in the *Methodology* volume edited by Shils, "The Meaning of 'Ethical Neutrality' in Sociology and Economics" (pp.1-47), should be recognized as one of Weber's much later studies and not part of the original methodological study. To fully understand Weber's methodological thought and its development, one should read the essays in the following order: (1) "Roscher's 'Historical Method' " (1903 [in *R & K*:55-91]); (2) " 'Objectivity' in Social Science and Social Policy" (1904 [in Weber 1949:49-112]); (3) "Knies and the Problem of Irrationality" (part 1, 1905 [in *R & K*:93-163]); (4) part 2 (1906 [in *R & K*:163-207]); (5) "The Logic of the Cultural Sciences" (1906 [in Weber 1949:113-88]); and (6) *Critique of Stammler* (1907 [1977]).

When the student of Weber proceeds in this fashion, she or he will find that there is far more to Weber's methodological thought than secondary accounts would have us believe. Furthermore, a "large number of epistemological questions which are far deeper than those raised" (Weber 1949:49) in the "Objectivity" essay are indeed raised and explored in the *Roscher and Knies* essays, as well as the *Critique of Stammler*. But more: students of Weber should not fail to notice that Weber's classical essay, *The Protestant Ethic and the Spirit of Capitalism* (1958a [1905]), was written and published while Weber was in the middle of his protracted study of the methodological foundations of the social sciences. Those wishing to find clues to Weber's notion of "causal explanation" hinted at in the *Protestant Ethic* should look to *Roscher and Knies* for vital clues.

Weber's (1981 [1913]) essay "On Some Categories of Interpretive Sociology" represents a later attempt to state his position more generally. But it is doubtful that a reader of that essay alone—or the opening methodological discussion of *Economy and Society* (Weber 1968:esp. 3-31), itself based on the former essay— will be able to grasp either the full range of the issues Weber was dealing with or the central logic of his position. It is only by means of the study of the early methodological essays as a whole that one can fully grasp the nature of Weber's unique conception of "causal explanation" and "teleological rational interpretation," and how these two are integrally connected with the study of all the forms of rationality and rationalism in comparative and historical perspective. Weber's notion of "rational interpretation," which included the idea that reasons and causes are related, had ultimately to result in the elaboration of typologies of "social action" or *culturally embedded* forms of *rationality.*[9] Although Weber (1981:159ff.) began to move in this direction in the "Categories" essay of 1913, this was not fully carried out until (probably) the last year of his life when he wrote what is called the "methodological introduction" to *Economy and Society* (1968:esp.3-62; and see Graber 1981). There one finds the clearest expression of the "types of social action" (see below, p. 67f), and these categories make the most sense when seen against the backdrop of Weber's methodological efforts to work out a framework for "rational interpretation" based on the conjuncture of (culturally) established meanings and motives.

The present study is perhaps a first chapter in a more adequate understanding of Max Weber's complex and still unsurpassed methodological probings. Perhaps we can look forward to a time when such an understanding will be joined by equally intense studies of Weber's substantive writings, especially those in the comparative historical sociology of religion. In the meantime it may be suggested that with this recovery of the wider dimensions of Weber's methodological thought we are in a very much enhanced position for rethinking the logic of explanation in sociology and the social sciences.

NOTES

1. While a great variety of philosophers of science participated in the discussions leading to the postempiricist shift, the critical essays and studies which served as the principal "exhibits" of contention included the following (in *rough* chronological order):

N.R. Hanson (1958) *Patterns of Discovery.*
——— (1961) "Is There a Logic of Discovery?"
——— (1963) *The Concept of the Positron.*
Karl Popper (1959) *The Logic of Scientific Discovery.*
——— (1968 [1963]) *Conjectures and Refutations.*
Thomas Kuhn (1962), *The Structure of Scientific Revolutions.*
P.K. Feyerabend (1962a) "Explanation, Reduction, Empiricism."
——— (1962b) "Problems of Microphysics."
——— (1964) "Realism and Instrumentalism."
——— (1965a) "Problems of Empiricism."
——— (1965b) "Reply to Criticism."
——— (1970) "Against Method: Outline of an Anarchist Theory of Knowledge."
Joseph Agassi (1963) *Towards an Historiography of Science.*
Imré Lakatos (1963/64) "Proofs and Refutations."
——— (1970) "Falsification and the Methodology of Scientific Research Programs."
——— (1976) "History of Science and Its Rational Reconstructions."

This is not intended to be an exhaustive list, but it does contain the studies in which the central issues precipitating postempiricist philosophy of science are most sharply stated. One can, however, point to the earlier work of V.O. Quine and N. Goodman, as well as Stephen Toulmin, though the former two would not be good examples of philosophers using *historical* insights.

2. Readers might think that it is unfair to judge students of Weber and the methodology of the social sciences writing before 1960 according to the lights of postempiricist philosophy of science. But this perspective *was* available in the writings of Peirce, Whewell, and others (including Weber) earlier in the century, but that is to anticipate our story.

3. I am assuming that the reader is aware of Popper's (and Hanson's) critique of induction as a method of discovery and that induction is not a candidate for this office. For additional critiques of induction see Whewell (in Butts, 1968, chs.4,5) and Peirce (1931-35, vol.5). For a discussion of these issues and an illustrative case study of the role of conjectures and abductive inference (as opposed to induction) in sociology, see Huff (1975).

4. One may also consult the study by David Haas (1982) which seems to demonstrate that even the most positivist-minded contemporary survey researchers do not attempt to employ "covering laws" in their explanations or generalizations. This is because their only information is based on historically located samples of social action and opinion, based on one society (the United States), frequently only one city, in one region of the country, and one point in time. This practical situation tells against the hypothetico-deductive model as an explanatory ideal.

5. The hermeneutic literature of the social sciences has now reached mammoth proportions. Aside from the work of Habermas and Gadamer, one should consult Hirsch (1967), Richard Palmer (1969), Ricoeur (1971, 1974), Von Wright (1971), and for an explication of Gadamer, David Hoy (1978). For an informed application of hermeneutics to the natural sciences, see Heelan (1972).

6. There is a voluminous literature that needs to be brought into discussions of observation, interpretation, and understanding of "meaning." The range of materials that one needs to be sensitive to extends from "Brain Mechanisms of Visual Attention" (Wurtz and others 1982), to *The Influence of Culture on Visual Perception* (Segall et al. 1966). The results of the latter study deserve greater attention by social scientists (p.214): "The findings we have reported, and the findings of others we have reviewed, point to the conclusion that to a substantial extent we learn to perceive; that in spite of the phenomenally absolute character of our perceptions, they are determined by perceptual inference habits; and that various inference habits are differentially likely in different societies."

   For a more recent test of the Segall thesis, see Wagner (1982). And for a different departure leading to similar conclusions, see the collection of essays assembled by Mary Douglas (1982). All of this—applied to our earlier context regarding the putative "laws of psychology"—would suggest that if there were such, they would be laws of *perception*, which, I take it, do not exist in a form applicable to social action.

7. According to Schutz: "It is the great contribution of Max Weber in his *verstehende Soziologie* to have given the principles of a method which attempts to explain all social phenomena in the broadest sense (thus all objects of the cultural sciences) in relation to the 'intended meaning' which the actor connects with his action" (1971, vol. 1:138). Yet, he continues, "it seems to me these methods can only become fully intelligible by means of far-reaching investigations of a constitutive phenomenology of the natural attitude. Such a science will find more than a guide in Husserl's investigations in the area of transcendental phenomenology" (pp. 138-39). In the light of our discussion to follow and Husserl's very different conception of "intentionality," this is an extraordinary claim. See below, for the differences regarding intentionality.

8. In a personal communication (January 1978) Professor Tenbruck affirmed that he does not now "hold the view on which my article of '59 ended." Tenbruck's turn toward the task of unraveling the wider thematic unity of Weber's substantive research is most welcome. But even his 1980 Prefatory Note to the translation of his paper on the thematic unity of Weber's work gives the reader the clear impression that Weber "moved from his methodology to a historical and cultural sociology" (Tenbruck 1980:313), as if Weber's methodological thought were neither related to nor foundational for the comparative historical approach that he pioneered. The point surely is that we must study both Weber's methodological essays and his comparative historical studies, and without such study we shall not be able to grasp the underlying logic of explanation that is implicit in his writings on religion, especially *The Protestant Ethic and the Spirit of Capitalism.*

9. Wolfgang Schluchter (1981:21) has recently suggested that "rationalism and rationality become essential subjects of investigation *only* because 'the development of inner-worldly and otherworldly values toward rationality, conscious endeavor and sublimation through knowledge' destroys the 'primeval naiveté' of human beings about themselves and the world. . . ." [my emphasis] While there is much to be said for this *historical* perspective, I suggest that it was an inherent part of Weber's explanatory framework (from *Roscher and Knies* onward) that the reasons and motives (which serve as causes of social action) were derivative components of the implicit 'rational' ordering of social action imposed by a *particular* culture. *The Protestant Ethic and the Spirit of Capitalism* is, of course, a prime substantive illustration of this methodological lesson. That "motives" are inherent *cultural* entities was recognized by Talcott Parsons in his Heidelberg address given just before his death: "That is, not only are there individualized motives peculiar to a particular actor, but there are internalized objects, norms, symbols, which are not peculiar to an individual actor, but which are part of the common culture. This notion opens up a very complex field of analysis. I think it is one of truly central attention in the most recent phases of theoretical development." (Parsons 1980:155).

REFERENCES

Agassi, Joseph (1963) "Towards an Historiography of Science," *History and Theory. Beiheft* 2, Middletown.

Best, R.A. (1975) "New Directions in Sociological Theory? A Critical Note on Phenomenological Sociology and Its Antecedents," *British Journal of Sociology* 26, 133-43.

——— (1978) "On Phenomenology and 'Phenomenological' Sociology," *British Journal of Sociology* 29, 121-24.

Bendix, Reinhard (1960) *Max Weber: An Intellectual Portrait.* New York.

Blackmore, John T. (1972) *Ernst Mach: His Work, Life and Influence.* Berkeley.

Brentano, Franz (1973) *Psychology from an Empirical Standpoint.* London.

Bridgman, Percy W. (1953) "The Logic of Modern Physics," in H. Feigl and M. Brodbeck (eds.), *Readings in the Philosophy of Science.* New York, pp. 34-46.

Bruun, H.H. (1972) *Science, Values, and Politics in Max Weber's Methodology.* Copenhagen.

Butts, Robert (ed.) (1968) *William Whewell's Theory of Scientific Method.* Pittsburgh.

Cohen, I.B. (1974a) "Newton's Theory vs. Kepler's Theory and Galileo's: An Example of a Difference Between a Philosophical and a Historical Analysis of Science," in Y. Elkana (ed.), *The Interaction between Science and Philosophy.* Atlantic Highlands, pp. 299-388.

——— (1974b) "History and the Philosophy of Science," in F. Suppe (ed.), *The Structure of Scientific Theories.* Urbana-Champagne, Illinois, pp. 308-49.

Davidson, Donald (1968) "Actions, Reasons, and Causes," in M. Brodbeck (ed.), *Readings in the Philosophy of the Social Sciences.* New York, pp. 44-58.

Davis, Martin (ed.) (1965) *The Undecidable.* Hewlett, New York.

Douglas, Mary (ed.) (1982) *Essays in the Sociology of Perception.* Boston.

Ermarth, Michael (1978) *Wilhelm Dilthey: The Critique of Historical Reason.* Chicago.

Farber, Marvin (1967) *The Foundations of Phenomenology.* Albany.

Feigl, Herbert (1969) "The Origin and Spirit of Logical Positivism," in P. Achinstein and S.F. Barker (eds.), *The Legacy of Logical Positivism.* Baltimore, pp. 3-24.

——— (1970) "The 'Orthodox' View of Theories: Remarks in Defense as well as Critique," in M. Radner and S. Winokur (eds.), *Minnesota Studies in the Philosophy of Science,* vol. 4. Minneapolis, pp. 3-16.

Feyerabend, Paul K. (1962a) "Explanation, Reduction, Empiricism," in Feigl and Maxwell (eds.), *Minnesota Studies in the Philosophy of Science,* vol. 3. Minneapolis, pp. 28-97.

——— (1962b) "Problems of Microphysics" in R. Colodny (ed.), *Frontiers of Science and Philosophy.* Pittsburgh, pp. 189-283.

——— (1964) "Realism and Instrumentalism: Comments on the Logic of Factual Support," in M. Bunge (ed.), *The Critical Approach to Science and Philosophy.* New York, pp. 280-308.

——— (1965a) "Problems of Empiricism," in R. Colodny (ed.), *Beyond the Edge of Certainty.* Pittsburgh, pp. 145-260.

——— (1965b) "Reply to Criticism," in R. Cohen and M. Wartofsky (eds.), *Boston Studies in the Philosophy of Science,* vol. 2. Dordrecht, pp. 223-61.

——— (1970) "Against Method: Outline of an Anarchistic Theory of Knowledge," in M. Radner and S. Winokur (eds.), *Minnesota Studies in the Philosophy of Science,* vol. 4. Minneapolis, pp. 17-130.

——— (1980) "Zahar on Mach, Einstein and Modern Science," *British Journal for the Philosophy of Science* 31, 273-82.

Gadamer, Hans-Georg (1975) *Truth and Method.* New York.

Gibbs, Jack (1972) *Sociological Theory Construction.* Hinsdale, Illinois.

Giedymin, Jerzy (1975) "Antipositivism in Contemporary Philosophy of Social Science and Humanities," *British Journal for the Philosophy of Science* 26 (Dec.), 276-301.

Gorman, R.A. (1975) "Alfred Schutz—An Exposition and Critique," *British Journal of Sociology* 26 (Mar.), 1-19.

Graber, Edith (1981) "Translator's Introduction to Max Weber's Essay on Some Categories of Interpretive Sociology," *The Sociological Quarterly* 22 (Spring), 145-50.

Haas, David F. (1982) "Survey Sampling and the Logic of Inference in Sociology," *The American Sociologist* 17 (May), 103-11.

Habermas, Jurgen (1971) *Knowledge and Human Interest.* Boston.

Hage, Gerald (1972) *Techniques and Problems of Theory Construction in Sociology.* New York.

Hanson, N.R. (1958) *Patterns of Discovery.* Cambridge.

——— (1961) "Is There a Logic of Scientific Discovery?" In H. Feigl and G. Maxwell (eds.), *Current Issues in the Philosophy of Science.* New York, pp. 20-35.

——— (1963) *The Concept of the Positron.* Cambridge.

——— (1967) "An Anatomy of Discovery," *The Journal of Philosophy* 64 (June), 321-52.

——— (1969) *Perception and Discovery.* San Francisco.

——— (1971) *Observation and Explanation*. New York.

Hart, H.L.A. and A.M. Honoré (1959) *Causation in the Law*. Oxford.

Heap, James L. and Phillip A. Roth (1973) "On Phenomenological Sociology," *American Sociological Review* 38 (June), 354-67.

Heelan, Patrick (1972) "Towards a Hermeneutic of Natural Science," *Journal of the British Society for Phenomenology* 3, 252-60.

Helmholtz, Hermann (1954) *On the Sensations of Tone as a Physiological Basis for the Theory of Music*. New York.

——— (1962) *Treatise on Optics*. 3 vols. New York.

Hempel, Carl (1965) *Aspects of Scientific Explanation*. New York.

——— (1972) *Fundamentals of Concept Formation in Empirical Science*. Chicago.

Hiebert, Erwin H. (1970) "The Genesis of Mach's Early Views on Atomism," in R. S. Cohen and R. Seeger (eds.), *Ernst Mach as Philosopher, Boston Studies in the Philosophy of Science*, vol. 6. Dordrecht, pp. 79-106.

Hirsch, Eric (1967) *Validity in Interpretation*. New Haven.

Holton, Gerald (1973) *Thematic Origins of Scientific Thought: Kepler to Einstein*. Cambridge.

Homans, George (1961) *Social Behavior: Its Elementary Forms*. New York.

——— (1964) "Contemporary Theory in Sociology," in Robert E.L. Faris (ed.), *Handbook of Modern Sociology*. Chicago, pp. 951-77.

——— (1967) *The Nature of Social Science*. New York.

Hoy, David Couzen (1978) *The Critical Circle: Literature, History and Philosophical Hermeneutics*. Berkeley.

Huff, Toby E. (1975) "Discovery and Explanation in Sociology: Durkheim on Suicide," *Philosophy of the Social Sciences* 5 (Sept.), 241-57.

Husserl, Edmund (1894) "Bericht über deutsche Schriften zur Logik aus dem Jahre 1894," *Archiv für Systematische Philosophie* 3, 216-44.

——— (1970 [1900]) *Logical Investigations*. 2 vols. New York.

——— (1931 [1913]) *Ideas: General Introduction to Pure Phenomenology*. London.

Kahl, Russell (ed.) (1971) *Selected Writings of Hermann von Helmholtz*. Middletown.

Kolakowski, Leszek (1969) *The Alienation of Reason: A History of Positivist Thought*. New York.

——— (1975) *Husserl and the Search for Certitude*. New Haven.

Kordig, Carl R. (1973) "Observational Invariance," *Philosophy of Science* 40 (Dec.), 558-69.

Kraft, Victor (1953) *The Vienna Circle: The Origins of Neo-Positivism*. New York.

Kuhn, Thomas (1962) *The Structure of Scientific Revolutions*. Chicago.

Lakatos, Imré (1963-64) "Proofs and Refutations," *British Journal for the Philosophy of Science* 14, 1-25; 120-39; 221-43; 296-342.

——— (1970) "Falsification and the Methodology of Scientific Research Programs," in Lakatos and Musgrave (eds.), *Criticism and the Growth of Knowledge*. Cambridge, pp. 91-195.

——— (1976) "History of Science and Its Rational Re-Constructions," in C. Howson (ed.), *Method and Appraisal in the Physical Sciences*. Cambridge, pp. 1-22.

Lenzer, Gertrud (ed.) (1975) *Auguste Comte and Positivism.* New York.

Lieberson, Jonathan (1982a) "The 'Truth' of Karl Popper," *New York Review* 29, 67-68.

——— (1982b) "The Romantic Rationalist," *New York Review* 29, 51-56.

Mach, Ernst (1960) *The Science of Mechanics.* Chicago.

Marshall, Gordon (1982) *In Search of the Spirit of Capitalism.* New York.

Maull, Nancy (1977) "Unifying Science Without Reduction," *Studies in the History and Philosophy of Science* 8, 143-62.

Merton, Robert K. (1968) *Social Theory and Social Structure.* New York.

Mises, Richard von (1951) *Positivism: A Study in Human Understanding.* New York.

Mill, John Stuart (1969 [1865]) *Auguste Comte and Positivism, Collected Works of John Stuart Mill,* vol. 10. Toronto, pp. 263-368.

Mullins, Nicholas (1974) "Theory Construction from Available Materials: A System for Organizing and Presenting Propositions," *American Journal of Sociology* 80 (July), 1-15.

Murch, Gerald M. (ed.) (1976) *Studies in Perception.* Indianapolis.

Nelson, Benjamin (1981) *On the Roads to Modernity: Conscience, Science, and Civilizations,* ed. T.E. Huff. Totowa.

Palmer, Richard E. (1969) *Hermeneutics. Interpretation Theory in Schleiermacher, Dilthey, Heidegger, and Gadamer.* Evanston.

Parsons, Talcott (1937) *The Structure of Social Action.* New York.

——— (1980) "On the Relation of the Theory of Action to Max Weber's *Verstehende Soziologie,*" in W. Schluchter (ed.), *Verhalten und System.* Frankfort am Main.

Passmore, John (1967) "Logical Positivism," in *The Encyclopedia of Philosophy,* vol. 5. New York, pp. 52-57.

Pastore, Nicholas (ed.) (1971) *Selective History of Theories of Visual Perception: 1650-1950.* New York.

Peirce, Charles Sanders (1931-35) *Collected Papers.* 6 vols. Cambridge, Mass.

Perinbanayagam, R. S. (1975) "The Significance of Others in the Thought of Alfred Schutz," *Sociological Quarterly* 16, 500-21.

Popkin, Richard (1964) *The History of Skepticism from Erasmus to Descartes.* New York.

——— (1965) "The High Road to Pyrrhonism," *American Philosophical Quarterly* 2, 1-15.

Popper, Karl (1959) *The Logic of Scientific Discovery.* New York.

——— (1968) *Conjectures and Refutations.* New York.

——— (1972) *Objective Knowledge.* New York.

——— (1976) *Unended Quest.* Chicago.

Reichenbach, Hans (1938) *Experience and Prediction.* Chicago.

Rickert, Heinrich (1894) "Zur Theorie der naturwissenschaftlichen Begriffsbildung," *Vierteljahrsschrift für wissenschaftliche Philosophie* 18, 277-319.

——— (1902) *Die Grenzen der Naturwissenschaftlichen Begriffsbildung.* Tübingen.

——— (1923-24) "Die Methode der Philosophie und das Unmittelbare," *Logos* 12, 235-80.

——— (1962 [1899]) *Science and History.* New York.

Ricoeur, Paul (1971) "The Model of the Text: Meaningful Action Considered as a Text," *Social Research* 39 (Autumn), 529-62.

———— (1974) *The Conflict of Interpretations.* Evanston.

Runciman, W.G. (1972) *A Critique of Max Weber's Philosophy of Science.* Cambridge.

Ryle, Gilbert (1971) *Collected Papers.* 2 vols. New York.

Scheffler, Israel (1967) *Science and Subjectivity.* Indianapolis.

Schiller, F.C.S. (1917) "Scientific Discovery and Logical Proof," in Charles Singer (ed.), *Studies in the History and Method of Science.* Oxford, pp. 235-89.

Schelting, Alexander von (1934) *Max Webers Wissenschaftslehre.* Tübingen.

Schluchter, Wolfgang (1981) *The Rise of Western Rationalism: Weber's Developmental History.* Berkeley.

Schutz, Alfred (1964-71) *Collected Papers.* 3 vols. Nijhoff.

———— (1967 [1934]) *The Phenomenology of the Social World.* Evanston, Illinois.

Segall, Marshall; Campbell, Don T.; Herskovits, M.J. (1966) *The Influence of Culture on Visual Perception.* Indianapolis.

Spiegelberg, Herbert (1971) *The Phenomenological Movement.* The Hague.

Suppe, Frederick (ed.) (1974) *The Structure of Scientific Theories.* Urbana-Champagne, Illinois.

Taylor, Charles (1971) "Interpretation and the Sciences of Man," *The Review of Metaphysics* 25, 3-51.

Tenbruck, Friedrich (1959) "Die Genesis der Methodologie Max Webers," *Kölner Zeitschrift für Soziologie und Sozialpsychologie* 11, 573-630.

———— (1980) "The Problem of Thematic Unity in the Work of Max Weber," *British Journal of Sociology* 31, 316-51.

Torrance, John (1974) "Max Weber: Methods and the Man," *European Journal of Sociology* 15, 127-65.

Turner, Herbert Hall (1963) *Astronomical Discovery.* Berkeley.

Vernon, M.D. (1952) *A Further Study of Visual Perception.* Cambridge.

Von Wright, Georg (1971) *Explanation and Understanding.* Ithaca.

Wagner, Daniel A. (1982) "Ontogeny in the Study of Culture and Perception," in D.A. Wagner and H.W. Stevenson (eds.), *Cultural Perspectives on Child Development.* San Francisco.

Weber, Max (1922) *Gesammelte Aufsätze zur Wissenschaftslehre.* Tübingen.

———— (1949) *The Methodology of the Social Sciences.* New York.

———— (1958a) *The Protestant Ethic and the Spirit of Capitalism.* New York.

———— (1958b) *The Rational and Social Foundations of Music.* New York.

———— (1968) *Economy and Society.* Totowa.

———— (1975) *Roscher and Knies: The Logical Problems of Historical Economics.* New York.

———— (1977) *Critique of Stammler.* New York.

———— (1981 [1913]) "Some Categories of Interpretive Sociology," *The Sociological Quarterly* 22 (Spring), 151-80.

Wilson, Curtis (1974) "Newton and Some Philosophers on Kepler's 'Laws.' " *Journal for the History of Ideas* 35 (April-May), 231-58.

Woodger, Joseph (1970) *The Techniques of Theory Construction.* Vol. 11, no. 5 of *International Encyclopedia of Unified Science.* Chicago.

Wurtz, Robert H.; Michael E. Goldberg; and David L. Robinson (1982) "Brain Mechanisms of Visual Attention," *Scientific American* 246, (June), 124-35.

Zetterberg, Hans (1955) "On Axiomatic Theories in Sociology," in P.F.

Lazarsfeld and M. Rosenberg (eds.), *The Language of Social Research.* New York, pp. 523-40.
——— (1965) *On Theory and Verification in Sociology.* Totowa.

CHAPTER ONE

INTRODUCTION

Between 1975 and 1979 a remarkable series of writings† on the methodology of the social sciences, written by Max Weber, George Simmel, and Wilhelm Dilthey, had been translated into English for the first time. These translations give us a vastly enriched conception of Weber's understanding of the social sciences and a glimmer of the nature of the *Methodenstreit*, the 'battle of the methods', which was carried on with great intensity by German social scientists primarily during the two decades which bracket the turn-of-the-century. But this 'battle' cannot be understood without taking into account the philosophical and scientific currents of at least the last quarter of the nineteenth century.

Each of the works listed merits special attention and evaluation. Yet after prolonged thinking about them, it seems to me that they are most fruitfully read and understood in the context of the *Methodenstreit* and its argumentative issues. Moreover, the claim that Simmel and Dilthey were major influences on Weber, even that Weber 'adopted the basic ideas' of Dilthey, for example, or that Weber was given his basic clues for the 'ideal type' by Simmel, is longstanding.

Furthermore there is a widespread view—a radically misconceived notion repeated on both sides of the Atlantic—that there is an 'intimate relationship' between Weber's 'interpretative sociology' and the perspectives of phenomenology. This fable is generally presented in one of two forms. On the one hand, it is claimed that Alfred Schutz used Husserl's phenomenology to 'correct' Weber who had naively overlooked some important methodological points (best left indefinite for the moment). Or on the other hand, it is boldly asserted, despite all of Husserl's protests to the contrary—that '*pure transcendental phenomenology will be established not as a science of facts, but as a science of essential Being*' (1931 [1913], p. 44; original emphasis)—that 'there is an intimate theoretical connection between the [Husserlian] demand "back to

---

† A discussion: Max Weber, *Roscher and Knies. The Logical Problems of Historical Economics*. Translated with an Introduction by Guy Oakes. New York: Free Press, 1975; Max Weber, *Critique of Stammler*. Translated with an Introductory Essay by Guy Oakes. New York: Free Press, 1977; Georg Simmel, *The Problems of the Philosophy of History*. Translated with an Introduction by Guy Oakes. New York: Free Press, 1977; *W. Dilthey, Selected Writings*. Selected, edited, and translated with an Introduction by H. P. Rickman. Cambridge: Cambridge University Press, 1976; and W. Dilthey, *Descriptive Psychology and Historical Understanding*, translated by R. M. Zaner and K. L. Heiges. The Hague: Nijhoff, 1977.

the things'' and the quest of *verstehende*, or ''understanding'' sociology, as implied in the definition by Max Weber...' (Wolff 1978, p. 501).

It is not an easy task to fathom the depths of Max Weber's methodological thinking, nor to follow the course of the *Methodenstreit*. But with the help of these new translations, a few secondary works, and some additional probing, we can now see that the assumptions above regarding Weber's position and influences on it are at least ninety degrees out of phase.

Despite the recent enthusiastic revival of interest in Dilthey's (and Simmel's) writings, Weber's methodological views were largely—and sometimes polemically—opposed to Dilthey's conceptions, and subsequently carried the day soon after their appearance (or so it appears). Likewise, Weber's appreciation of Simmel's brilliance notwithstanding, his views stand at odds with Simmel both methodologically and substantively. A glimmer of Weber's misgivings about Simmel's conception of sociology was revealed quite recently with the translation and belated publication of Weber's incomplete analysis of Simmel's work (see Weber 1972). Doutless Weber's methodological writings are considered nonpareil, though I believe their full significance has not been appreciated even by Weber's most attentive and thorough-going students. In any event, I hope to offer evidence for the justice of this view.

In the present essay I shall attempt to set out and elaborate the methodological position which Weber began to work out as he undertook his methodological study called *Roscher and Knies. The Logical Problems of Historical Economics* (1975 [1903-06], hereafter *R & K*). In doing so I shall suggest that Weber's actual methodological views (*a*) are very close to the spirit of what is now called 'post-empiricist' philosophy of science; (*b*) reject the alleged differences between the 'logic' (or methodology) of the social and natural sciences; and (*c*) represent a viable position which is both foundational for the methodology of the social sciences and consistent with recent developments in the logic of explanation in the social sciences as found in the work of Hart and Honoré (1959), Davidson (1968), White (1965) and others.

To facilitate this discussion I shall first briefly sketch some themes of the *Methodenstreit*. Then I shall schematically set out Weber's position. Following that I shall present some details of Weber's position as he argued it. At that point it will be obvious where Weber stood *vis-à-vis* Dilthey (and the 'new' hermeneutics) as well as 'phenomenological sociology'.

THE BATTLE OF THE METHODS

The *Methodenstreit* in German social science erupted in 1883 with the simultaneous publication of methodological works which took up contrasting and antagonistic standpoints. One of these was Carl Menger's, *Untersuchungen über die Methode der Sozialwissenschaften und der politischen Oekonomie insbesondere* (translated into English as *Problems of Economics and Sociology*, 1963). The other work was Wilhelm Dilthey's *Introduction to the Human Studies* (the so-called *Einleitung* of which only the 'Preface' plus a few pages is available in English translation in the Rickman volume, pp. 159-67). But it was not the clash of *these* two perspectives which initially caused so much clamour. It was instead the clash between the representatives of the 'classical' and 'historical' schools of economics. The former was represeted by Menger and the latter by Roscher, Knies, and Gustav Schmoller. 'The temperature of the methodological controversy in economics', Webers tells us two decades after the event, reached its peak in the 1880s as 'a consequence of Menger's [*Problems of Economics and Sociology*], Schmoller's review of Menger's book, and Menger's furious response' (*R & K*, p. 94).

At issue were two sets of problems which ought to be carefully kept in mind. On the one hand, there was the question of what *model* of scientific knowledge ought to be the goal of 'historical economics', 'the moral sciences', or 'the cultural sciences'. The pro-naturalist (or naturalist) view was that the pursuit of 'natural laws' ought to be the goal of all the sciences. Yet at the same time there seemed to be a disjuncture between understanding the 'concrete' historical phenomenon or event and the 'laws' of history which were postulated. There was a peculiar conception according to which the 'collective' life of society was law-governed while the domain of the 'individual' was 'irrational' because of 'free-will'. The 'historical school' (as represented by Roscher, Knies, and Schmoller) had particular difficulty in articulating the opposed theoretical goals of seeking to establish 'natural laws' (which they curiously accepted) on the one hand, and describing the unique 'concrete', and allegedly 'irrational', behavior of the 'individual' on the other.

Menger's position was clearly naturalistic and 'nomological'. He gave a strong and central role to *theoretical* understanding at all levels. According to Menger:

we understand a concrete phenomenon [not only 'historically' but] in a *theoretical* way (on the basis of the corresponding sciences) by recognizing it to be a special case of a certain regularity (conformity to law) in the succession, or the coexistence of phenomena. In other words, we become aware of the basis of the existence and the peculiarity of the nature of a concrete phenomenon by learning to recognize in it merely the exemplification of a conformity-to-law of phenomena in general. [1963, pp. 44-45; original emphasis.]

This view seems surprisingly modern, largely because it seems to follow John Stuart Mill. But additional problems arose—at least in Weber's mind—about the 'laws of nature' as well as the supposed 'laws of human thought' which were taken to be the subject matter of that 'auxiliary' but indispensable 'science of the mind', psychology. The view still persists, Weber lamented in 1904:

which claims that the task of psychology is to play a role comparable to mathematics for the *Geisteswissenschaften* in the sense that it analyzes the complicated phenomena of social life into their psychic conditions and effects, reduces them to their most elementary possible psychic factors and then analyzes their functional interdependence. Thereby, a sort of 'chemistry' if not 'mechanics' of the psychic foundations of social life would be created. [1949, pp. 74-75.]

In this connection, then, we ought to stress the fact that it was John Stuart Mill who clearly formulated this idea that the 'general laws of mind' are foundational entities for the 'moral sciences'. The logic of the moral sciences in Mill's scheme rested upon:

the laws of formation of character [which] are, in short, derivative laws, resulting from the general laws of mind, and are obtained by supposing any given set of circumstances, and then considering what, according to the laws of mind, will be the influence of those circumstances on the formation of character. [Mill 1965, p. 46.]

Consequently it is important to bear in mind that this image of a science of the 'laws of mind' as a handmaiden to the *Geisteswissenschaften* permeated the thought of all those who wrote about the methodology of the sociocultural sciences in the late nineteenth century. Not suprisingly, it was also opposed by Durkheim (1938, pp. 97ff.).

The 'historical school' of economics tried to display the changing character of historical evolution and thus of human 'psychology'. But as Weber perceived (in *R & K*), the historical school was also caught in a Hegelian web of 'emanationism' according to which the 'laws of history' unfold and become actualized in the 'concrete'. Thus while the historical school rightly sought to reveal the historically contingent and conditioned aspects of economic life (in contrast to the 'natural law' model of Menger and classical economics), Max Weber could not identify with its exponents because of this curious mixture of Hegelian 'panlogism' (to use Weber's term) and the Marxian 'materialist conception'. Weber simply did not believe in the 'laws of history', whether Hegelian or Marxist. But Weber apparently saw Hegel's panlogism as the most 'mischievous'. This reaction to Hegel served to reinforce Weber's philosophical 'instrumentalism': the view that the concepts of science are only useful 'instruments' which can never be said to be either 'historical reality not even the "true" reality' (Weber 1949 [1904], p. 93).

However, the notion of 'laws of thought', which in Hegelian philosophy could be said to be evolving, were perceived rather differently among the proponents of the *Geisteswissenschaften*. This side of the *Methodenstreit*, which came alive with Rickert and Weber, may be identified with Wilhelm Dilthey.

Dilthey's *Einleitung,* or *Introduction to the Human Studies* (Dilthey 1922-24, vol. 1), was a work Weber generously described as 'the first comprehensive outline of a logic of the *non*-natural sciences' (*R & K*, p. 94). For even later champions of Dilthey have suggested that the *Einleitung* 'remained a fragment' (Rickman 1976, p. 157). Moreover, Dilthey's early involvement in the most severe positivist experimental psychology is well known (see Ermarth 1978, pp. 31ff., 64ff.).

In any event, Dilthey did initiate a distinctive approach to the 'human studies'. Insofar as methodological issues are concerned, however, far more significance is to be attributed to Dilthey's 'Ideas Concerning a Descriptive and Analytic Psychology' (1894), the first of the two essays edited and translated by Zaner and Heiges in *Descriptive Psychology and Historical Understanding*. (Rickman has also included excerpts from this piece in his volume.) Additionally, the preliminary study called 'The Development of Hermeneutics' (1900, and fully translated by Rickman) merits reading.

In these essays Dilthey sought to provide a new foundation for the *Geisteswissenschaften*, the 'human studies'. In doing so he accepted the notion that some sort of 'psychology' would provide the firm foundation for the human studies. In short, Dilthey proposed a 'descriptive psychology' which would set aside 'explanatory' psychology and at the same time obviate the need for such uncertain things as 'hypotheses'. Dilthey's lament was, 'Hypotheses, everywhere only hypotheses!' (1977, p. 27). Consequently, Dilthey proposed a method of direct, immediate, and undistorted access to the world of 'inner' human experience. Thus the 'explanation' of *nature* was contrasted with the 'understanding' of *human* life and its expressions (Dilthey in Rickman 1976, pp. 89, 248). In the end, the result was to be 'not a purely "logical" distinction [but] an "ontological" dichotomy' (Weber in *R & K*, p. 216 *n*22). And this was indeed the view accepted by Weber's purposefully chosen opponents, that is, Gottl, Münsterberg, Lipps, Croce and some others criticized in *Roscher and Knies*.

However, in order to understand these moves on Dilthey's part, we must take into consideration the beginnings of the phenomenological movement, which, as everybody knows (e.g., Farber 1967; Spiegelberg 1971; Ryle 1971, vol. 1), began, not with Husserl in 1900 (or in 1913), but in the 1870's with Franz Brentano. It was he who initiated the effort to fashion a 'descriptive psychology' or 'phenomenology', primarily in his *Psychology from an Empirical Standpoint* (1973 [1874]). Three attributes of this movement in particular ought to be noted.

First, Brentano's enterprise was declared to be a new *empirical* inquiry; it was an *empiricist* departure which displayed all the rhetoric of neo-Baconianism proclaiming the need to 'get to the facts', free and unhampered by theoretical obstacles or 'prejudiced minds'. Secondly, this empiricism was a radical sensationalism (cf. Agassi 1966), a claim to have direct and incontestable access to the sensibilia of mental life. But these sensibilia were wholly internal. Brentano claimed that we have 'inner perception' of mental ('psychic') phenomena which has a remarkable 'distinguishing characteristic: its immediate, infallible self-evidence' (Brentano 1973, p. 91). Thus 'inner experience' is seemingly both the tool and the object of investigation of this new 'descriptive psychology'. Through 'inner experience' descriptive psychology arrives at *general truths* directly; in Brentano's words, arrives 'at one stroke and without induction' (as cited by Kraus in Brentano 1973, p. 370). In this connection it is not without importance that Brentano opposed the theory of perception of Helmholtz who referred both to the effects of learning and of 'unconscious inference' on perception. Whereas Helmholtz took the view that 'the sensations [of perception] are signs to our consciousness, and it is the task of our intelligence to learn their meaning' (as cited in Hanson 1958, p. 177 n2; and see Helmholtz 1963, vol. 3), Brentano sided with the 'nativists' (especially Hering [see Woodward 1978 and Richards 1977]) who believed in automatic mechanisms of apprehension. For them, there was no such thing as 'unconscious' or delayed inference. Inner perception (*innere Wahrnehmung*) was immediate (*unmittelbare*; Brentano 1874, p. 119).

But finally—and this has repeatedly been overlooked by social scientists eager to embrace phenomenology—Brentano invented a radically different conception of 'intentionality'. 'Intentionality' in Brentano's work does *not* imply any actual 'intention' on the part of the actor in the sense of having a 'purpose', 'aim', or 'goal'. The '*intentio*' inside the intending being, Spiegelberg has pointed out, 'is precisely [the] conception which Brentano himself did not share' and which led him later to drop the notion of 'intentionality' altogether (1971, p. 40). In other words, Brentano's actors were removed from *cultural* backgrounds, from 'purposes' (or intentions) and 'motives'. If actors did have such things, it was not part of 'descriptive psychology' to investigate them. It could study the 'contents' of mental life 'directly'. And therefore, we should remember in the future that, 'it was certainly none of Brentano's doing that this new wholly unscholastic conception came to sail under the old flag of "intentionality"' (Spiegelberg 1971, p. 41).[1]

There has been a neglect of Brentano's influence on Dilthey, and that is a

---

1 The literature on the history of the concept of 'intentionality', especially in connection with Brentano, is now substantial. See the essays collected in McAlister (1976) as well as Hedweg (1979).

serious omission. It is reasonably clear, once one has been alerted to the clue, that Brentano's influence on Dilthey began early and ran deep. Dilthey's writings as early as 1875 contain references to Brentano's *Psychology* (see Dilthey 1922-24, vol. 5, p. 55; and Ermarth 1978, p. 369 *n*21). All of Dilthey's theoretical works appear to reflect this insistence on 'inner experience' as the tool of the 'human studies'. For example, the 'Preface' to Dilthey's 1883 'Einleitung' displays this priority of 'inner experience' as the unspoiled and infallible access point to reality: 'undiluted reality only exists for us in the facts of consciousness given in inner experience' [*inneren Erfahrung*] (in Rickman, p. 161).

In brief, Dilthey took over in a rather strong sense the sensationalist and psychologistic epistemological position of Brentano. That in itself should indicate why Weber could not have adopted Dilthey's 'basic ideas'. For in addition to being a Kantian in epistemological matters, Weber was widely read in the philosophy of science of his day, and whether or not he had read Helmholtz's treatise on physiological optics, Weber knew many of Helmholtz's other writings and drew on them freely in his methodological writings, in his book on *The Rational and Social Foundations of Music* (1958), and in other places.

We see, then, that Dilthey's project for a 'descriptive psychology' must be viewed in the context of the early phenomenological movement and the work of Brentano. In addition to establishing a new foundation for the human studies, Dilthey also believed that these notions about 'inner perception' provided the key to solving the riddle of the relations between psychology and epistemology. Through the analysis of 'inner experience', in which the connections of mental life were said to be given immediatley and directly, as a lived experience (*unmittelbar, lebendig als erlebte realität* [Dilthey 1922-24, vol. 5, p. 151; 1977, p. 35]), 'one can resolve the problem of the relationship of epistemology and psychology' (1977, p. 35). And this was to be carried out through the elaboration of a 'descriptive psychology' (1977, p. 35).

But with the publication of the 'Ideas' essay, Dilthey met his Waterloo. For the Berlin psychologist Ebbinghaus wrote a devastating essay, published the following year, in which he mercilessly attacked Dilthey's position (Ebbinghaus 1895). As Michael Ermarth has pointed out, 'The crux of Ebbinghaus's scathing critique concerned the doctrine of the self-givenness of the psychic coherence' (1978, p. 184). Ebbinghaus challenged the immediacy of the apprehension of 'mental connections' and argued that in the domain of mental life there is the same use of 'hypotheses' as in any other domain of science. Here we need not go into the details, but simply note, in Weber's words, that Dilthey was 'decisively rejected by the psychologists' (*R & K*, p. 250 *n*46). Weber adds to this note, ten years after the event, that Dilthey's account in the 'Ideas' essay is 'weakened by the following prejudice: the belief that specific systematic *sciences* must correspond to certain formal categories of knowledge' (original emphasis).

But Ebbinghaus's onslaught was only one of the blows which defeated Dilthey's position. For the next significant attack was launched by Heinrich Rickert in his *Die Grenzen der naturwissenschaftenlichen Begriffsbildung* ('The Limits of Concept Formation in the Natural Sciences', 1902), a book Weber wrote, which 'can be conceived as an attack on Dilthey's position'. 'It is astonishing', Weber continues, 'that many "sociologists" continue to overlook this point, a species of their blind enthusiasm' (*R & K*, p. 240 *n*16).

In short, Dilthey was devastated both theoretically and personally by this attack, and he consequently gave up teaching psychology, went back to his historical inquiries, and even avoided friendly colleagues such as William James who had invited him to an international conference (see Ermarth 1978, p. 185). It is not surprising, therefore, that in *R & K* Weber (in opposition to Dilthey) declared his affinities with the methodological position set out by Rickert:

> The point of view fundamental to the present study is close to Rickert's in the following respect: we both claim that 'mental' [*psychischen*] or 'intellectual' [*geistige*] phenomena—regardless of how these terms are defined—are just as susceptible as 'dead' nature to an analysis in terms of abstract concepts and laws. The modest degree to which strictness can be attained and the limitations upon quantifiability are not a consequence of properties peculiar to the 'mental' or 'intellectual' objects of the concepts and laws in question. [P. 216f. *n*22.]

This brief sketch should serve to give some perspective on the issues and the drift of the *Methodenstreit* prior to Weber's entrance into it. Weber saw the situation as one in which two equally objectionable methodological positions—a naturalistic and an anti-naturalistic stance—had been argued. And Weber could not wholeheartedly join forces with either one.

On the one hand, the naturalist camp seemed to espouse a 'naturalistic monism' which for Weber was that 'wrong-headed view [whose exponents] are still playing variations on the theme, that "scientific knowledge" is identical with the "discovery of laws"' (1949[1906], p. 163 *n*30). This naturalistic prejudice—a thinly veiled reference to the philosophy of Mill—made it appear 'as if there is in general no conceivable meaning of scientific work other than the discovery of the *laws* of events' (1949 [1904], p. 86). And Weber saw 'this will-to-believe of naturalistic monism' in both the historical and classical schools of economics: that is, in the work of Menger as well as in the work of Roscher, Knies, and Schmoller. However, in the case of the historical school, the naturalistic prejudice was reinforced by ideas drawn from another quarter, that is, the 'emanationist' theory of Hegel. In the work of both Roscher and Knies, the idea of a 'Volk' as a set of 'instinctual forces' located outside history, yet animating it, seemed to Weber to represent an illustration of the influence of Hegel (see *R & K* pp. 66ff. and 202-207). Aside from this confluence of Hegelian emanationism and naturalistic monism, Weber's reasons for rejecting the 'monism' have not been studied, very largely because of the persistence of logical positivist sympathies among social scientists and philosophers of the social scientists.

On the other hand, the anti-naturalist partisans in the *Methodenstreit* were arrayed around a sensationalist epistemology—as outlined above—according to which we have direct, 'unmediated', access to the meaning and significance of human experience and expression. This assumption allegedly set off the 'human studies' from 'the sciences', both 'logically' and 'ontologically'. Logically it was claimed that our direct access to meaning and significance meant that there was no need to use 'hypotheses' but that one arrived at 'knowledge' in one leap. Furthermore, the notions of 'inner experience' (*inneren Erfahrung*) and 're-living' (*nacherleben*) led to the assertion that the subject matter of the *Geistes-wissenschaften* is ontologically separate from experience of the natural world.

But in addition to this, it bears repeating that Brentano's innovation regarding the concept of 'intentionality' prevented those attached to it from attempting to formulate a position according to which the 'meaning' of any oral or written expression could be decoded by reference to the actor's 'motives' and 'intentions' which themselves would necessarily be tied to cultural settings. Consequently, 'purposes', 'reasons', and 'motives' were bracketed and the only access to human 'meanings' was via 'direct' and 'unmediated' (*unmittelbar*) 're-living' (*nacherleben*) of 'mental connections'. Weber's '*verstehende* sociology' had nothing to do with these psychologistic and sensationalist assumptions (as even a reading of 'Ueber einige Kategorien der verstehenden Soziologie' [1913] reveals).

In short, when Weber began writing his methodological essays about 1902, he was well appraised of the developments in phenomenology and the writings on 'hermeneutics', especially Dilthey's paper on the rise of hermeneutics mentioned above.

WEBER AND THE METHODOLOGICAL UNITY OF THE SCIENCES

In *Roscher and Knies* (a set of three essays begun in 1902 and published in 1903, 1905, and 1906), we find Max Weber completely rethinking the methodology of the social sciences. To do so, he had to deal with all the fundamental questions about 'laws' and 'causality', prediction and the alleged 'irrationality' of human action, the difference between 'self-evidence' and 'validity', the nature of 'understanding' and 'interpretation', and of course aspects of the problem of the construction of 'ideal types'. All of these issues are dealt with in *R & K*, although Weber's first and most important discussion of ideal types occurs in the 1904 essay called ' "Objectivity" in Social Science and Social Policy'. The nature of ideal types and their use is also significantly advanced in the 1906 essay titled 'Critical Studies in the Logic of the Cultural Sciences', especially in the second part of the essay. Additionally, in the *Critique of Stammler* (1977 [1907]) Weber discusses a number of related issues concerning 'rule-governed' behaviour.

In brief, between 1903 and 1907 Weber published just short of 450 pages (in English translation) on methodological problems. But that enumeration falls short of mentioning the over three hundred additional pages he wrote on the problems of survey research and analysis, 'marginal utility' theory, and the 'energetic' theory of culture (of Ostwald) which appeared between 1907 and 1909. All of this ought to put to rest the quite mistaken notion that Weber either did not or was reluctant to examine the fundamental methodological/epistemological foundations of the social sciences, a view fostered by Alfred Schutz (1967, p. 7).[2]

Moreover, given this extensive array of methodological problems, it is not surprising that Weber plunged deeply into the writings of the philosophers, scientists, and 'logicians of science' of his day. In addition to the writings of Hermann von Helmholtz, Weber read Mach's *Analysis of Sensations* (1914 [1886]), Wundt's discussion of the changing status of the axioms of mechanics, von Kries on probability theory, as well as Mill, Husserl, Avenarius, and probably the logician Sigwart who had an important influence on Rickert.

In the present discussion I shall focus on the perspectives of *R & K* and attempt to show the ways in which Weber's position radically differed from Dilthey's, and also some ways in which it differed from Simmel's thinking. At

---

2 That it was Schutz and not Weber who failed to provide a 'thorough undergirding of his results by a secure overall philosophical point of view' (Schutz 1967, p. 7), will become increasingly evident as this essay proceeds. See notes 9 and 10 to Part II of this essay.

the same time, it will be possible to see the necessity to understand *R & K* in order to grasp the epistemological underpinnings of Weber's other essays, especially the famous 'Objectivity' essay, as well as the 'Critical Studies in the Logic of the Cultural Sciences'. Indeed, Weber alerts the reader of 'Objectivity' that 'a systematic inquiry would require the treatment of a large number of epistemological questions which are far deeper than those raised here' (1949, p. 49). Hence it is in *R & K* where Weber took up these 'far deeper' questions. In doing so, he worked out a methodological view which not only rejected Dilthey's position, but also significantly qualified the 'nomological' model of explanation, yet preserved 'causal' explanation. Schematically, Weber's methodological view contains the following elements:

(1) a critique of the limits of 'nomological' explanation in the *natural* sciences;

(2) a displacement of the 'natural law' model of explanation in social science by a 'causal' explanatory model which characterizes 'motives' as 'causes';

(3) This latter pattern of explanation entails (*a*) the notion that the 'interpretation' of social action requires the decoding of 'meaning'; (*b*) this in turn requires the consideration of 'motives', 'purposes', and 'intentions' as the key to understanding the 'meaning' of action; (*c*) 'the rules of the game', and ethical and practical 'maxims' serve as 'causal' factors 'determining the course' of social action;

(4) due to the above, the discovery of 'meaning', i.e., 'understanding' and 'interpreting' is logically (or epistemologically) *no* different than the discovery of 'laws' and 'causes' in the physical world; both rely upon the use of hypotheses and the 'instruments of concept formation';

(5) in all domains of knowledge there is a difference between 'experience' and 'knowledge'; consequently the role of 'intuition' in the genesis of hypotheses is the same in all domains of knowledge; likewise the testing (or verification) of hypothetical claims is logically the same in all domains of knowledge.

THE NOMOLOGICAL MODEL

Max Weber's decision to take up the 'logical problems of historical economics' appears to have been influenced by two events. Marianne Weber tells us, 'The Heidelberg *Philosophische Facultät* planned to issue a jubilee volume on the occasion of an anniversary of the university, and Weber was urged to contribute to it' (1975, p. 259). The invitation seems to have been issued in 1902, and Weber ultimately wrote the essays called *Roscher and Knies*—although he could not finish them on time and therefore published them independently. His decision to take up methodological issues was probably influenced by the appearance early in 1902 of the complete study by Heinrich Rickert called *The Limits of Concept Formation in the Natural Sciences*, the first part of which was published in 1896. Weber read the whole study in April of 1902, and wrote to Marianne: 'I have finished Rickert. He is *very* good; in large part I find in him the thoughts I have had myself, though not in logically finished form. I have reservations about his terminology' (p. 260 in Marianne Weber 1975). All of this fits well with Weber's avowed purpose in writing the study, namely, 'to test the value of his [Rickert's] ideas for the methodology of economics' (*R & K*, p. 213 *n*9).

Once launched on this enterprise, Weber found this 'incidental study' to be a 'burden and a torment' as well as a bottomless pit of methodological issues which he found himself persistently writing about until at least 1909, and again in 1913.

Viewed programmatically, R & K first focusses on conceptions of science and the place of 'laws' in historical explanation. In the second and third installments, Weber shifts attention to what we may call the 'anti-naturalist' view and the manifold contemporary notions about 'understanding' and 'interpretation'. Although the range of issues and authors to which Weber devotes attention is perplexing for the reader, one cannot escape the impression that Weber had a well-laid-out plan in view. At the same time, one cannot fail to note that Weber was undermining positions which continue to be championed today in the social sciences. In particular, he criticized the positivist conception of science aimed at establishing 'laws' and 'correlations', as well as the (now very popular) view that the social sciences (or 'human studies') are uniquely 'interpretative'. Similarly, one can find in R & K discussions which attack the validity of the claim that psychological investigation (now called 'genetic epistemology') provides a firm foundation for mapping a unilinear pattern of cognitive development characterized by the indubitable recognition of 'higher' moral standards. This critique is found in Weber's discussion of Wundt.

In the first installment, 'Roscher's "Historical Method"', Weber subjects the methodological assumptions of nineteenth century historical economics to rigorous scrutiny. In the second installment, 'Knies and the Problem of Irrationality', Weber continues his elucidation of the methodological assumptions which guided historical economics. For the first forty or more pages (pp. 55-101), Weber seems to be setting out the underlying assumptions which most need to be considered. As in the case of Knies's work, Weber tells us that first, one 'must separate intertwined strands of ideas which, as it might be put, come from different balls of yarn. This accomplished, he must then systematize each of these collections of ideas independently' (p. 95).

In broad strokes, the following themes may be identified as the crucial issues in the first third of the study which focusses on Roscher and Knies: (1) What is the role of 'natural laws' in historical explanation? (2) How does the avowed *historical* task of exhaustive description of the particularities of human existence and events align with causal analysis? (3) Is human action 'irrational' and unpredictable as a result of 'free will', and if so, how then do 'natural laws'—of the 'economy' in Roscher's case—and the as yet *undiscovered* 'laws of mind' (of psychology or social psychology) apply to human conduct and historical evolution?

In this effort to set out Weber's programme of methodological inquiry, I shall deliberately avoid prolonged discussion of a number of important epistemological issues because they are clouded by problems of translation. In a great many passages, we find Weber referring to 'concrete' events, 'personalities', mass movements, and the like. Just why the translator (Guy Oakes) chose 'concrete' in all these cases—especially where the German is *individueller*—is not clear. In philosophical discussions, the contrast was frequently made between 'abstract' and 'concrete', but philosophically informed writers—and I include Weber among them—realize that all 'concrete' descriptions involve theoretical (and hence 'abstract') concepts. It would seem to make better sense to render *individueller Begriffe* (p. 65) as 'individual' (or 'particular') concepts than as 'concrete concepts' in the light of Weber's sensitivity to the problem of 'the *"hiatus irrationalis"* between concepts and reality' (p. 66).

A problem of equal significance is the notion of 'value relations'—*Werte auf Beziehung* and other *Wert* words—which Oakes has rendered as 'axiological' without alerting the reader to this innovation, nor giving the slightest justification for the rendering (which appears to issue from the work of von Schelting [1934] and Bruun [1972]). Likewise, there are many renderings of *Beziehung auf Werte* ('value relations') as 'axiological' (as on pp. 239 *n*11 and 246 *n*30, etc.) which are not listed in the index.

Finally, we should note that the term *spezifische* (p. 58) has been rendered as 'definitive' when the footnote attached to the term in Weber's text (1922, p. 6 *n*1) suggests a far more qualified adjective.

In 'Roscher's "Historical Method"' Weber highlights the problems of adopting the *naturalistic* 'method' of scientific practice for use in the 'historical' sciences. In doing so, Weber points to the contradictions in Roscher's self-declared aims while he examines the limits of natural science itself.

Since Roscher calls his method 'historical', Weber tells us, it must share 'the scientific aims and the methodological tools of the historical sciences. Its exclusive project must be the intuitive reproduction of the total reality of economic life' (p. 58). Such a programme of detailed description would seem to be at odds with 'the goal of classical economics: to discover in the multiplicity of events the lawlike and uniform rule of simple forces'. Yet surprisingly Roscher takes it as his task to provide just those 'laws' of history; he even sees his task as the establishment of 'evolutionary laws of *historical* change' (p. 60).

Hence it seems that Roscher wants to study the historically *unique* and contingent, yet he imagines that this leads to the formulation of 'natural laws'. To this Weber responds:

genuine 'natural laws' of the behavior of phenomena can be formulated only on the basis of analytical abstraction which eliminates the 'historically contingent'. Therefore it must follow that the ultimate goal of economics is the formation of a system of abstract and analytical laws, a system of maximal logical completeness in which concrete *'contingencies'* have been, as much as possible, stripped away. But this appears to be precisely the goal that Roscher has rejected in principle. [P. 59.]

But according to Weber's analysis, Roscher has not abandoned the search for the 'system of laws' which guide both history and the economy, but rather he has abandoned the study of the characteristically *meaningful* dimensions of historical reality which make it important to *us* and hence worthy of study.

Roscher's means for achieving this system of laws is connected with his notion of discovering historical 'parallelisms' or 'correlations'.[3] This comes out in the discussion of the concept of 'Volk': 'an intuitable totality, the cultural bearer of a

---

3 Here and elsewhere Oakes has translated *'Parallelismen'* as 'correlations'. Nowadays 'correlations' imply a form of statistical analysis which does not seem to apply to Roscher's 'historical' work. The translators of Menger's *Problems of Economics and Sociology* (1963, pp. 118ff.) rendered the term as used in Menger's discussion of Roscher as 'parallelisms'. I have frequently substituted 'parallelisms' for 'correlations' in these citations. Nevertheless, when Weber refers to situations involving 'large numbers' it may be correct to translate the term as 'correlations'.

meaningful total essence' (p. 62). Roscher hoped to produce a large number of 'parallelisms' from the study of a large number of observations about different 'Volk'. Eventually, he imagined, these parallelisms or analogies would 'be elevated to the logical status of "natural laws" which hold for all members of the class "Volk"' (p. 63). But Weber dismisses this. On the one hand, he is willing to grant that in 'individual cases, a complex of regularities discovered in this fashion may have extraordinary heuristic value'. But, on the other hand, Weber points with surprising boldness to a defect:

it should be obvious that [this discovery of parallelisms] cannot be conceived as the ultimate *goal* of any science: neither a 'nomological' nor an 'historical' scheme, neither a 'natural' science nor a 'sociocultural' science. [*Geisteswissenschaft*.] [P. 63.]

But on second thought, Weber's brilliance here can be said to be a rejection of the view that 'laws' in science are but summary statements of observations. In that sense Weber's declaration might be read as a criticism of inductivism. According to J. S. Mill, for example, 'the expression, Laws of Nature, *means* nothing but the uniformities which exist among natural phenomena (or, in other words, the results of induction), when reduced to their simplest expression' (1973, p. 318; original emphasis). But Weber argues differently:

Let us grant that these disciplines could establish an enormous number of 'empirical' historical generalizations. Nevertheless, these generalizations would have no *causal* status. Correlations of this sort could only constitute a subject matter of a scientific investigation, an investigation which would begin only after these correlations had been established. At this point—and this is most important—the investigation would have to produce a decision concerning the following issue: what *sort* of knowledge should be the aim of investigation? [Pp. 63-64.]

This point of view therefore has much in common with that of C. S. Peirce, who in reply to certain necessitarian arguments concluded, 'a uniformity, or law, *is par excellence*, the thing that requires explanation' (1931-35, vol.6, p.612). Thus Weber puts us on notice that whatever 'empirical generalizations' might emerge out of research *must themselves* be explained—not simply organized into shopping lists—according to principles that are by no means self-evidently reflected in the phenomena themselves.

Moreover, perhaps we may say that it is at this point that Weber begins to launch his attack on what has come to be called the 'hypothetico-deductive', or covering law model of explanation (Popper 1959; Hempel and Oppenheim 1953). As we saw earlier Carl Menger had put forth a view similar to this. Menger's conception of the task of science is that familiar one of subsuming particular instances or events under 'covering' principles of 'lawful' regularity.

However, Weber qualified this model in three directions. *First*, he notes that not all empirical regularities are 'causal' principles; *second*, a scheme of completely deductive statements becomes (by design) 'increasingly alienated from empirically intelligible reality' (p. 64) so that it becomes questionable as to whether or not one is actually in an explanatory sense 'deducing' the 'concrete' event or an *idealized* conception of it. In Kantian fashion, Weber may have construed laws as the 'form' of existence which obviously could not provide the 'content' of 'concrete' existence. Furthermore, as an *historical* discipline, historical economics must seek to uncover the particularity of economic phenomena in their geographical and temporal settings. If 'natural laws' are to be involved, they cannot be conceived as devices which allow the 'deduction' of all the individual specificity of historical periods and their characteristics. Since 'laws' are by nature conceptual formulations which extend infinitely beyond any particular setting, there are limits to which such laws may be construed as 'descriptions' of particular events. Accordingly, Weber asserts that Roscher's version of the deductive nomological model:

is not only empirically impossible. Because of the nature of nomological knowledge, it is also logically impossible. The formation of 'laws'—relational concepts of general validity—is identical with the progressive depletion of conceptual content through abstraction. The postulate of the 'deduction' of the content of reality from general concepts... is logically absurd. [P. 218 *n*23.]

Likewise, Weber criticizes Gustav Schmoller's version of the natural science model, according to which, 'Every completed science is deductive. For as soon as the basic elements are completely determined, even the most complicated phenomena can only be a combination of these elements' (as cited by Weber, p. 218 *n*23). To this claim Weber responds, 'In my view this claim grants what does not even hold in the most specialized spheres of the employment of exact nomological concepts'.

Finally, Weber introduces a different order of considerations. The pursuit of parallelisms and covariations raises the question: 'what sort of knowledge should be the aim of the investigation?' (p. 64). In doing so Weber contrasts the production of formulae—mathematical expressions of statistical regularities—with the *understanding* of reality. Suppose, Weber suggests, that the historical disciplines 'attempt to *understand* reality' (original emphasis). In that case it would seem that we should want to deal with 'the characteristic *meaning* of single, concrete cultural elements together with their concrete causes and effects' (p. 65). If that were the case, then the establishment of parallelisms would be at best 'one among many possible techniques for forming individual concepts [*individueller Begriffe*]'. In other words:

there is *a priori* not the slightest reason to believe that the *meaningful* and essential aspects of concrete patterns would be identified by the abstract concepts of the correlations.... In consequence: it obviously does not make sense to suppose that the ultimate *purpose* of concept formation in the historical sciences could be the deductive arrangement of concepts and laws—discovered by employing correlations [*Parallelismen*]—under other concepts and laws of increasingly general validity and abstract content. [Pp. 65-66.]

At this point Weber has arrived at his unique vantage point for elaborating a new conception of the tasks and goals of the cultural sciences. Moreover, it is one which rests on a different conception of *causality* (on which, more below). Yet, instead of concluding his critique of the nomological model as applied in the natural sciences, and explicitly stating the implications of his evolving view—that which requires attention to the 'meaning' of sociocultural process—Weber offers an elucidation of the Hegelian elements in Roscher's historical methodology (pp. 66-73 as well as pp. 89-91). The point of this is to show that behind Roscher's notion of 'Volks' as coherent unities in historical process there is both an organicism and an Hegelian emanationism. According to Weber:

the Hegelian theory of concepts... attempts to surmount the '*hiatus irrationalis*' between concept and reality by the use of 'general' concepts—concepts which, as metaphysical realities, comprehend and imply individual things and events as their instances of *realiza-tion*. [P. 66.]

Weber is willing to grant a 'logical' validity to this view:

Given this 'emanatist' conception of the nature and validity of the 'ultimate' concepts, the view of the relation between concept and reality as strictly *rational* is logically unobjec-tionable. On the one hand, reality is comprehended in a thoroughly perceptual fashion: with the *ascent* to the concepts, reality loses none of its perceptual content. The maximization of the content and the maximization of the extension of concepts are, therefore, not mutually unsatisfiable conditions. In fact, they are mutually inclusive. This is because the 'single case' is not only a member of the class, but also a part of the whole which the concept represents.... [P. 66.]

What Weber here calls 'emanatism' is probably close to Popper's notion of 'essentialism' (cf. Popper 1968, pp. 103ff.). However, the point of Weber's discussion is obviously to show that while Roscher's position is distinct from Hegel's in many respects, this 'emanatist' view of concepts and reality lies behind much of Roscher's methodological thinking. The concept of a '*Volks-geist*', for example,

is treated as a real, uniform entity which has a metaphysical status. It is not the *result* of countless cultural influences. Just to the contrary, it is viewed as the *actual ground* of all the individual cultural manifestations of a Volk, the source from which they all emanate. [P. 61; original emphasis.]

In short, the Volk and the Volksgeist become metaphysical entities outside of history, yet animating history.

Weber then turns to the work of Karl Knies, and he does so it seems, primarily out of deference to his reputation *and* because one finds in Knies's work an agenda of methodological issues which remain to be adequately resolved. For while Knies subscribed to the views of natural science found in Roscher, Knies abandoned 'the distinction between purposeful human action, on the one hand, and the natural and historical conditions for this action, on the other' (p. 96). In place of it, Knies adopted a scheme based on the idea of 'the "free" and therefore *irrational-concrete*, action of persons, on the one hand', and the nomological determination of natural events, including the human economy, on the other. In short, the same problem met with in Roscher of the complete determination of natural processes confronted with the (now explicitly stated) 'irrationality' of human action comes sharply to the fore.

In Weber's mind, this contrast 'between the "creative" significance of the acting personality and the "mechanical" causality of natural events' (p. 98) was a repeated contrast 'which has been "solved" hundreds of times, only to reemerge in a new guise' (p. 98). For this reason, Weber found 'some justifica-tion for going somewhat further into these issues and attempting to clarify this problem'. When Weber's discussion thereafter soon leaves Knies far behind, we begin to appreciate what Weber meant when he suggested that readers will suspect that 'I am using Knies only as a "pretext" in order to discuss the problems raised here' (p. 237 *n*3). For we may also note that both the second and third installments of the study are titled, 'Knies and the Irrationality Problem', even though a scant sixteen pages (six at the outset and the last ten) are devoted to Knies's work. In this subtle fashion, Weber suggests that the many theories of 'understanding' and 'interpretation' proposed by Münsterberg, Gottl, Lipps,

Croce (and Dilthey) are but additional variations on the theme of the 'irrationality' of human life and action, and therefore presumably testify to the need for a radical separation of the methodology of the social sciences from that of the natural sciences.

From this point forward, Weber's strategy is designed to probe these two notions of the singularity of the 'creative' nature of human personalities (and psychic life) as opposed to the 'mechanical' operation of natural processes. While carrying this analysis forward, Weber fashions ingenious arguments which at once limit the applicability of the idea of the complete mechanical operation of nature *and* the notion of the 'irrationality' and incalculability of human action. Consequently, the completion of Weber's critique of the limits of nomological explanation follows his discussion of the new defense of the idea of 'creative synthesis' in the work of Wilhelm Wundt.

REFERENCES

Agassi, Joseph (1966) 'Sensationalism', *Mind*, **75**, 1-24.
Brentano, Franz (1874) *Psychologie vom empirischen Standpunkt*. Leipzig.
————— (1973) *Psychology from an Empirical Standpoint*. London.
Bruun, H. H. (1972) *Science, Values, and Politics in Max Weber's Methodology*. Copenhagen.
Davidson, Donald (1968) 'Actions, Reasons, and Causes', in May Brodbeck (ed.), *Readings in the Philosophy of the Social Sciences*. New York, pp. 44-58.
Dilthey, Wilhelm (1922-24) *Gesammelte Schriften*, vols. 1 and 5. Leipzig.
Durkheim, Emile (1938) *The Rules of Sociological Method*. New York.
Ebbinghaus, H. (1895) 'Ueber erklärende und beschreibende Psychologie', *Zeitschrift fur Psychologie der Sinnesorgane*, **9**, 161-205.
Ermarth, Michael (1978) *Wilhelm Dilthey. The Critique of Historical Reason*. Chicago.
Farber, Marvin (1967) *The Foundations of Phenomenology*. Albany.
Hanson, N. R. (1958) *Patterns of Discovery*. Cambridge.
Hart, H. L. A. and A. M. Honoré (1959) *Causation in the Law*. Oxford.
Hedweg, Klaus (1979) 'Intention: Outline for the History of a Phenomenological Concept', *Philosophy and Phenomenological Research*, **39**, 326-40.
Helmholtz, Hermann (1962) *Treatise on Physiological Optics*, 3 vols. New York.
Hempel, Carl and Paul Oppenheim (1953) 'The Logic of Explanation', in H. Feigl and M. Brodbeck (eds.), *Readings in the Philosophy of Science*. New York, pp. 319-52.
Husserl, Edmund (1931) *Ideas. General Introduction to Pure Phenomenology*. London.
McAlister, Linda (ed.) (1976) *The Philosophy of Brentano*. London.
Mach, Ernst (1914) *The Analysis of Sensations and the Relation of the Physical to the Psychical*. Chicago.
Menger, Carl (1963) *Problems of Economics and Sociology*. Urbana.
Mill, John Stuart (1965) *On the Logic of the Moral Sciences*. Indianapolis.
————— (1973) *A System of Logic*, vols. 7 and 8 of *The Collected Works of John Stuart Mill*. Toronto.
Peirce, C. S. (1931-35) *Collected Papers*, 6 vols. Cambridge, Mass.
Popper, Karl (1959) *The Logic of Scientific Discovery*. New York.
————— (1962) *The Open Society and Its Enemies*, 2 vols. New York.
————— (1968) *Conjectures and Refutations*. New York.
————— (1974) *Objective Knowledge*. New York.
Richards, Joan (1977) 'The Evolution of Empiricism: Hermann von Helmholtz and the Foundations of Geometry', *British Journal for the Philosophy of Science*, **28**, 235-53.

Rickert, Heinrich (1902) *Die Grenzen der naturwissenschaftlichen Begriffsbildung*. Tübingen.

Ryle, Gilbert (1971) *Collected Papers*, 2 vols. New York.

Schutz, Alfred (1967) *The Phenomenology of the Social World*. Evanston, Ill.

von Schelting, Alexander (1934) *Max Webers Wissenschaftslehre*. Tübingen.

Spiegelberg, Herbert (1971) *The Phenomenological Movement*. The Hague.

Weber, Marianne (1975) *Max Weber. A Biography*. New York.

Weber, Max (1913) 'Ueber einige Kategorien der verstehenden Soziologie', *Logos*, 4, 253-94.

———— (1922) *Gesammelte Aufsätze zur Wissenschaftslehre*. Tübingen.

———— (1949) *The Methodology of the Social Sciences*. New York.

———— (1958) *The Rational and Social Foundations of Music*. Carbondale.

———— (1972) 'Georg Simmel as Sociologist', *Social Research*, 39, 155-63.

White, Morton (1965) *Foundations of Historical Knowledge*. New York.

Wolff, Kurt (1978) 'Phenomenology and Sociology', in T. Bottomore and R. Nisbet (eds.), *A History of Sociological Analysis*. New York, pp. 499-556.

Woodward, William R. (1978) 'From Association to Gestalt: The Fate of Hermann Lotze's Theory of Spatial Perception', *Isis*, 69, 572-87.

CHAPTER TWO

THE PROBLEM OF THE 'IRRATIONALITY' OF HUMAN ACTION

According to Wilhelm Dilthey, Wundt's notion of a 'creative synthesis' represents a new conception of mental life which foretells the demise of 'explanatory and constructive psychology' (1977, p. 49). Weber, however, saw things differently. In Weber's reading of Wundt, the latter subscribed to the notion that the domain of mental life was uniquely 'creative', even though for Wundt mental events were strictly causally determined. Despite this strict determinism, Wundt found something uniquely new and 'creative' issued from mental events which 'is not contained *in*' the component elements of the events themselves (as cited in *R & K*, pp. 107 and 105). There is a 'creative synthesis' according to which the whole is quite different from the properties of its part.

To Weber, this Wundtian thesis had all the markings of a 'value judgment'. Aside from the possibility of describing some personalities as 'creative', Weber warns that:

we must be extremely careful to employ [this idea of 'creative'] in such a way that it designates something besides the precipitate of *valuation* [*Wertung*] which we project onto causal factors and the effects we ascribe to them. [P.101.]

Consequently, Weber declares 'wholly mistaken' that view according to which

the 'creative' properties of human action are correlated with 'objective' variations in the properties of causal relations. That is to say, correlated with those properties which are *independent* of our evaluation, which are in or deducible from empirical reality. [P. 101.]

Hence, that which identifies what is 'creative' is nothing other than our own value assessments.

From a logical point of view, the physical and chemical processes which produce a seam of coal or a diamond constitute a 'creative synthesis' in the same sense as the chain of motives which link the intuitions of a prophet to the formation of a new religion. The two sorts of 'creative synthesis' can be substantively differentiated only by reference to differences in the predominant values in terms of which we conceive them. [P. 102.]

In other words, viewed *strictly* as a sequence of events and processes, both the production of a 'seam of coal' and a 'new religious inspiration' are equally 'creative' or equally insignificant, depending upon our value commitments. This line of reasoning urges Weber to make the point that it is precisely the *value* related qualities which constitute the historical interest. It is the variational differences created by *value relations* [*Wertbeziehungen*][4] which are of decisive

---

4 Oakes has translated the terms '*Wertbeziehung*', '*Beziehung auf Werte*', and sometimes '*Wertideen*', and related *Werte* compounds as 'axiological' without giving the

43

importance. 'This is why reflection concerning value relevance is the ultimate basis of the historical interest' (p. 102).

Accordingly, attention on the part of the historical researcher to particular value relations in some cases will lead to insignificant outcomes; in others very significant results will issue. In this latter case, 'new value connections' which had not before been noticed will be established. In the last analysis, 'differences in causal status as *differences* in *value* relations [*Wert*ungleichung] is the definitive category of the cultural sciences. This is the only possible meaning', Weber asserts, 'of the claim that "creative synthesis" is a phenomenon peculiar to the domain of the cultural sciences—a domain which may include specific mental events, cultural relations, or both' (p. 104; 1922, p. 51; original emphasis).

This is an important section of *Roscher and Knies* to understand and we should ponder the implications of translating the term *Wertbeiziehung* as 'axiological'. It is not only the fact that there may be *unexpected* behavioural and cognitive outcomes from a set of *value* commitments, such as the 'elective affinities' between Calvinist commitments and the 'spirit of capitalism'. But also, as we shall see, if a 'causal *interpretation*' of social action involves the uncovering of the *motives* and *intentions* of historical actors, then clearly it is the *value commitments* (not 'axiological' connections) which establish such motivational schemes. Moreover, Weber is not interested in a theory of values ('axiology'), but in the *cultural* commitments which motivate actors.

It should be noticed in this same section that Weber does not fail to emphasize that despite the researcher's attention to values, or better, 'meaning', there is no reason why 'mental events' cannot be studied 'independent of all value relations' [*Wertbeziehungen*] in the same manner as the natural event. This may seem to be an inelegant form of expression on Weber's part, a statement contradicting the notion that the researcher's starting point is with value commitments in the first place. However, Weber's desire is to reject the conclusion drawn by Dilthey and many others who were committed to what I shall call the 'descriptive psychology' school. Thus Weber wishes to assert that even though one recognizes the valuational stance of historical actors, there is no *logical* reason why human action cannot be analyzed in precisely the same fashion as any constellation of events in natural science. 'There is no reason at all why these series of changes [in mental events]—absolutely without exception and in exactly the same sense—cannot be subjected to a "value-free" conception, just like any other series of qualitative changes in "dead" nature' (p. 107).

Having disposed of the new defense of the presumably unique status of the study of human conduct based on this 'psychological' conception of the 'creative synthesis', Weber turns to Knies's version of the 'irrationality' thesis.

'In the opinion of Knies, and many others today', Weber wrote, the idea of 'free will' implies a radical 'irrationality' or 'incalculability' of human action (p. 120). In dealing with this thesis Weber deployed ingenious arguments which reflect both a deep appreciation of the patterns of social life and the nature and limits of natural science. In the first place, Weber argued:

---

reader any warning of this departure (and not only in those places listed in the index [i.e., pp. 102-104, 119, 145, 151, 181], but also on pp. 239, n. .12; 246, n. 30; 250, n. 43; 252, n. 47, and 259, n. 89). As far as I can determine, there is no warrant for this translation, and it misleadingly changes Weber's meaning as it seems to me. 'Axiology' is the translation given by Shils and Finch for '*Wertphilosophie*', but which is, Weber tells us, 'experienced' concrete reality contains no trace at all of a species of 'incalculability' peculiar to human conduct. Every military order, every criminal law, in fact every remark that we make in conversation with others, 'counts' on the fact that certain impressions will penetrate the 'psyche' of those for whom they are intended. They do not depend upon the absolute unambiguity of these impressions in every case. But they do depend upon a calculability which is sufficient *for the purposes* which the command, the law, and the concrete utterance are intended to serve. From a logical point of view, these calculations are no different from the 'statical' computations of a bridge builder, the agricultural economist, and the physiological hunches of a stock breeder. [Pp. 120-21; original emphasis.]

Thus from a *logical* point of view there is no 'difference between these cases and "natural processes"'.

If, on the other hand, 'calculability' is taken to mean 'predictable', then we can see the limits of the prediction of singular events in the natural sciences. For the '"calculability" of "natural processes" in the domain of "weather forecasting", for example, is far from being as "certain" as the "calculation" of the conduct of a person with whom we are acquainted' (p. 121). Moreover, imagine the challenge to natural science—Weber continues—to predict when and where a bolt of lightning might strike, how many pieces into which a boulder would be split, at what angle, where they will fall, with how many fragments, in what clusters (pp. 122-23). According to Weber, these problems represent an illustration of the degree to which *natural* events can be said to be 'irrational' and 'incalculable', despite the fact that they do *not* contradict any known nomological regularities. Weber raises doubts about whether or not in this case an explanatory 'causal regress' could be carried out, 'not only because these aspects of the event are absolutely "incalculable"—since their concrete determinants are lost without a trace', but also because 'such a causal "regress" would be quite "pointless"' (p. 122).

But more importantly, Weber suggests that at best all that can be achieved in such cases is an 'interpretation' [*interpretiert*], one 'which does not directly contradict our nomological knowledge'. This would be the case not only in the example of the splitting boulder, but in that such as phylogenesis. 'The main reason is', Weber says, 'that we can not now—and perhaps can never—acquire more knowledge' about the underlying processes (p. 123). Moreover, if the 'explanation' of the shattering of the boulder consists only in providing an 'interpretation' which is consistent with our nomological knowledge, this 'is an extremely imprecise form of causal explanation'. 'It *excludes* all empirically grounded necessary truth. In such an explanation, the universal validity of "determinism" remains purely *a priori*' (p. 123).

In these few lines, Weber has set out an impressive philosophy of nature which implies the notion of the radical incompleteness of all scientific knowledge. But Weber implies more. On the one hand, he seems to anticipate the widespread view developed in the nineteen thirties among philosophers of science that all scientific laws are in fact statistical or *probabilistic* (cf. Reichenbach 1938). On

---

'not in the methodology of the empirical disciplines' (1949, p. 12). Weber did not attempt to produce a 'theory of values', and it is too schematic to treat 'value relations' as 'axiomatic'. The precedent for this 'unhappy' term is Bruun (1972, pp. 147ff.) who seemingly took a cue from von Schelting (1934, p. 22).

the other hand, Weber sharply accentuates a view that is to be found in both C. S. Peirce and Popper according to which the universe is ruled not only by a high degree of regularity, but also by 'chance' (Popper 1974, p. 213). As Peirce put it:

Those observations which are generally adduced in favor of mechanical causation simply prove that there is an element of regularity in nature and have no bearing whatever upon the question of whether such regularity is exact and universal or not. Nay, in regard to *exactitude*, all observation is directly *opposed* to it.... Try to verify any law of nature, and you will find that the more precise your observations, the more certain they will be to show irregular departures from the law.... Trace their causes back far enough and you will be forced to admit they are always due to arbitrary determination, or chance. [1934-35, vol. 6, p. 46; original emphasis.]

Weber, however, uses his neo-Kantian background to suggest that in the analysis of any event, 'like *every* individual event, no matter how simple it may appear, [there is] an intensively *infinite* multiplicity of properties—if, that is, one *chooses* to conceive it in this way' (p. 124). According to this view, there ought to be an infinite number of hypotheses which might be applicable in any given situation. Thus, in the case of the fractured boulder, '[f]urther inquiry into the event would reveal a number of possibly relevant causal factors which "could be made larger than any given number, no matter how large"' (p. 124), and that, one may say, adds a radical *relativity* to the notion of the 'exact' natural sciences. Such a view is not distant from that spirit which conceives of the inevitability of 'paradigm shifts' as a major constituent of science. It is, furthermore, a proto-type of that view, championed by Popper, Feyerabend and others, that any set of observational statements may be deductive consequences of *more than one* theory (even *incompatible* theories; cf. Feyerabend 1962).

If then one compares the rock-fracturing with a case of relevant historically situated human action, if one considers 'the course of a change within the social relations of groups, a change which is produced by the complex interrelations of many particular individuals' (p. 124), one is led to admit that judging the degree of complexity to be greater in one case or the other is impossible. For given the infinity of physical hypotheses that might be entertained in the one case, 'no matter how complex a course of human "action" may be, "objectively" it is in principle impossible to include *more* "elements" than could be identified in this simple event in the physical world' (p. 124).

With this, Weber concludes his comparison of the irrationality of 'concrete human action and concrete natural events'. But this does not dispose of all the arguments alleging a peculiar irrational dimension in human experience. But it does bring Weber to the point of specifying the *qualitative* difference which in Weber's mind separates the form of *causal* explanation in the social sciences from that of the natural sciences:

In the analysis of human conduct, our criteria for causal explanation can be satisfied in a fashion which is qualitatively quite different. At the same time, this gives a qualitatively different shading to the meaning of the concept of irrationality. As regards the interpretation of human conduct, we can, at least in principle, set ourselves the goal not only of representing it as 'possible'—'comprehensible', in the sense of being consistent with our nomological knowledge. We can also attempt to 'understand' [*Verstehen*] it: that is to identify a concrete 'motive' or complex of motives 'reproducible in inner experience' [*nacherlebbares*], a motive to which we can attribute the conduct in question with a degree of precision that is dependent on our source material. In other words, because of its susceptibility to a meaningful *interpretation* [*Deutbarkeit*]—and to the extent that it is susceptible to this sort of interpretation—individual human conduct is in principle intrinsically less 'irrational' than the individual natural event. . . .[I]f human conduct cannot be interpreted in this way, it is no different from the fall of the boulder from the cliff. In other words, 'incalculability'—in the sense of the nonsatisfaction of the conditions for this sort of interpretation—is the principle of the 'madman'. [P. 125.]

In short, for Weber, 'causal' explanation involves both the 'interpretation' of *meaning* and the presupposition of regularity. Hence, Weber uses the notion of the 'interpretability' of human conduct to argue, (*a*) that this possibility separates human events from mere physical occurrences, and (*b*) that human conduct may in fact be conceived to be *less* 'irrational' than natural events. However, the apprehension of 'meaning' here is linked to the uncovering of a 'motive' (or complex of motives) which could be said to have prompted the action. If this kind of 'interpretation' were not possible, then human conduct would be 'no different from the fall of the boulder from the cliff'.

By this means, Weber radically alters our conception of 'causal' explanation in social science. 'Motives', which can here be assimilated to 'reasons', serve as the 'causes' of social action—a view which has only recently been given attention by philosophers of the social sciences (see Hart and Honoré 1959; Davidson 1968; and Ayer 1964, among others).

The possibility, however, of misconstruing Weber's position here and drawing the unwarranted conclusion that Weber meant to imply that *only* 'social' action has 'meaning' and hence requires a special method is very great. And this possibility is exacerbated by the translator's rendering *Spezifikum* as 'definitive' in the footnote where Weber first introduces this notion of the 'meaningful interpretation' of human conduct (p. 218, n.22; 1922, pp. 12-13, n.1).

Yet in the *Critique of Stammler*, Weber argued that 'meaning' is not an exclusive property of 'social' relations. This was illustrated in the case of the 'bookmark'. Any object which serves as a bookmark has 'symbolic value', that is, 'meaning'. But 'independent of the knowledge of this meaning, the bookmark is both useless and meaningless to me' (1977, p. 109). At the same time Weber pointed out that in the case of the use of a bookmark, 'no "social" relation of any sort is established in this case' (pp. 109-10). Following this example, Weber further elaborates his point with the following discussion:

Suppose that for conceptual purposes we distinguish the 'meaning' which we find 'expressed' in an object or process from all the other components of the object or process which remain after this 'meaning' is abstracted from it. And suppose that we define the sort of inquiry that is *exclusively* concerned with this set of components as 'naturalistic'. The result is still another concept of 'nature'. . . . In this sense of 'nature', nature is the domain of the 'meaningless'. Or, more precisely, an item *becomes* a part of 'nature' *if* we cannot raise the question: What is its 'meaning'? Therefore it is self-evident that the polar antithesis of 'nature' as the 'meaningless' is not 'social life', but rather the 'meaningful': that is, the 'meaning' ascribed to a process or object, the 'meaning' which *can* 'be found in it'. This includes, at one extreme the metaphysical 'meaning' of the cosmos as seen from the perspective of a certain system of religious dogmatics. At another extreme, it includes the 'meaning' which the barking of Robinson Crusoe's dog 'has' when a wolf approaches. Therefore we have shown that there is no sense in which the property of being 'meaningful'—the property of 'meaning' or 'signifying' something—is a feature peculiar to 'social' life, its definitive property. [Pp. 110f.; original emphasis.]

This rendering of Weber's German may be somewhat free, but Weber's argument is certainly evident; namely, that the property of being 'meaningful' is 'by no means exclusively characteristic of "social" life'.

If we now return to Weber's discussion in *R & K*, we see at once that it is not the attribute of having 'meaning' per se which Weber accented. It is on the contrary, the combined notions of 'motives' and 'intentions' [*Absichten*]. It is one thing to speak of the 'meaning' of some object or process, but it is quite another possibility to speak of the *motive* or *intention* of somebody. One can talk of the 'meaning' of 'nature' or whatever, but one cannot refer to the 'motive' of 'nature', or of some inanimate process. Furthermore, this is another aspect of Weber's altered conception of 'causal *interpretation*'. To explain or interpret some human action is to interpret the 'meaning' by supplying a 'motive'. The motive in this sense would be constituted by a set of 'reasons' and/or 'purposes' for the action. As we shall see, this results in Weber's conception of 'teleologically rational behaviour'.

In brief, the trajectory of Weber's critique of his predecessors, Roscher and Knies, has led him to fashion a 'qualitatively' distinct criterion which characterizes 'causal' explanation in the sociocultural sciences. By insisting that there must be a 'meaningful interpretation' [*sinnvollen Deutung*] in terms of *motives* and *intentions*, Weber has drastically modified the 'postivist' covering-law model of scientific explanation. And he adamantly rejected the possibility of using 'an empirical-statistical demonstration of the strictest sort' (p. 128) as a *substitute* for a meaningful interpretation which would reveal the connection between the actor's conduct and his 'intentions and beliefs' [*Absichten und Einsichten*] (p. 127). Weber does not attempt, however, to spell out here the differences and connections between motives and intentions. But he does later assert that 'ethical maxims' and the 'rules of the game' serve as 'causes' in human conduct. Weber saw no logical difference between the single case and 'large numbers'. In a particular case, such as the life of Friedrich II in the year 1756, we can understand it both as 'nomologically possible' and 'also as "teleologically" rational' (p. 127). But this does not result in the establishment of 'a statement of *necessity*', but on the contrary, we recognize 'that his conduct has an "adequate cause". I.e., given certain intentions and (true or false) beliefs of the monarch, and given also a rational action determined thereby, a "sufficient" motivation can be identified' (p. 127; original emphasis). Viewed 'purely from the point of view of the mode of satisfaction of criteria for causal explanation, cases concerning "interpretable processes" are no different from cases concerning "large numbers"'. This explanatory schema, therefore, yields a unique fusion of the methods of 'interpretive understanding' *and* 'causal' analysis.

Due to this need to supply accounts of the actor's motives and intentions, Weber insists that, 'Phenomenologically, "interpretation" [*Deutung*] simply does not fall under the category of subsumption under generalization' (p. 241, n. 24). Furthermore, by virtue of this qualification of the notion of 'causal' explanation, Weber can insist that '"laws" are intrinsically of absolutely no "significance" for the interpretation of "action"' (p. 128). For present purposes we need not debate the issues further.

Having raised the issue of what 'interpretation' in science might be, Weber is now prepared to consider the thesis that human 'experience' constitutes a range of phenomena which are fundamentally different from natural phenomena. According to one version of the thesis, human life and 'mental' events represent another kind of 'being' (*Sein*), and therefore require special modes of cognition. Such a view is an early product of one strand of phenomenology which culminates in the work of Heidegger.

UNDERSTANDING AND INTERPRETATION I

Throughout the early modern history of science it was a widely held view that scientific practice involves 'interpretation'. This was so above all because of the metaphor known as 'the Book of Nature' (on which see Nelson 1975). Even when Galileo launched his polemical debates defending the virtues of his methods and discoveries—about which he claimed demonstrable certainty—he was prone to refer to 'the open book of heaven', which unerringly told the truth (see Drake 1957, p. 196). Moreover, 'this grand book, the universe . . . cannot be understood unless one first learns to comprehend the language and read the letters in which it is composed. It is written in the language of mathematics, and its characters are triangles, circles, and other geometric figures' (p. 237f.).

In short, the metaphor of *nature* as a *text* which had to be deciphered and interpreted was central to the whole history of Western science. Consequently, Sir Francis Bacon subtitled his *New Organon*, 'True Directions Concerning the Interpretation of Nature'. The novelty of Bacon's grand instauration was his claim to having discovered infallible methods for guiding the mind in this interpretation, so that 'the mind itself be from the very outset not left to take its own course, but guided at every step; and the business be done as if by machinery' (1960, p. 34).

Likewise, the great nineteenth century philosopher and historian of science, William Whewell, while tempering Bacon's belief in the possibility of 'an art of discovery', gave us the aphorism, 'Man is the interpreter of nature; science is the right interpretation' (1840, vol. I, p. xvii).

Yet at the very moment when Whewell's humane and historically informed view of science was being set out, the rise of positivism in France and the spirit of empiricism in British thought gained the upper hand. The rhetoric of positivism declared that true science was based on direct 'observation' and the elimination of all metaphysics and 'speculation'. The result was an image of *natural science* as a set of directly apprehended, incontestable truths. When John Stuart Mill advocated the application of 'the methods successfully followed' in the natural sciences to 'the proper study of mankind' (1965, p. 6), the image of science and the methods invoked were precisely those associated with positivism. And Mill offered not a few words of praise for Comte himself (though Mill later regretted some of this).

But our story concerns late nineteenth century 'human studies' in Germany. If as Weber suggests, Dilthey's *Einleitung* was 'the first comprehensive outline of a logic of the *non*natural sciences' in Germany, it must also be said that Dilthey—perhaps unwittingly—contributed to the acceptance of the positivist mythos of natural science. For in the Preface to the *Einleitung,* he tells us that his 'starting point is the scientific approach. As long as it remains conscious of its limitations, its results are incontestable' (in Rickman, p. 164). Secondly, in accepting this myth of the infallibility of natural science, Dilthey rejected the idea of the *interpretation* of nature. 'Understanding [*verstehen*] of nature—*interpretatio naturae*—is a figurative expression' (p. 248), Dilthey tells us.

It is difficult to grasp the logic of Dilthey's severance of the modes of understanding here, for he also tells us that 'we call the process by which we recognize some inner content from signs received by the senses *understanding*' (original emphasis). Yet the signs of the heavens, the open book of the universe in Galileo's sense, are external stimuli which register on our retinas and generate internal sensations which, as Helmholtz put it, 'are signs to our consciousness, and it is the task of our intelligence to learn to understand their meaning'. In other words, Dilthey did not provide a *logical* separation of the modes of 'understanding' between the social and natural sciences, but (unknowingly) gave us precisely the sort of formulation which would, with only a little exposure to the history of the natural sciences, reveal their inherent *unity* of 'method'. Furthermore, since it is not easy to defend a *logical* separation of the processes of understanding and interpretation which operate in the social and natural sciences, Dilthey and all of his followers were forced into declaring an ontological separation of the modes of understanding of the various sciences.

As we saw earlier (ch. 1, pp. 31ff) the foundation for this ontological leap is to be found in the work of Franz Brentano, who delineated a unique domain of 'inner experience', a domain of inner 'psychic' experience, the special realm, Dilthey tells us, in which we can achieve an immediate and undistorted cognition of reality.

When Weber turns to 'Epistemological Discussions of the "Category" of "Interpretation' " [*Deutung*] in *Roscher and Knies,* all of those issues come dramatically into view. Yet it is not Dilthey's work which occupies Weber's attention. I would suggest that Weber omits direct discussion of Dilthey (except in footnotes) for two reasons. The first was Dilthey's public defeat (and personal humiliation) in the eighteen-nineties brought about by Ebbinghaus's attack, as well as the criticism of Rickert and Wundt. Secondly, Dilthey's workmanlike attachment to history prevented him from ever formulating sharp conceptual ideas and working them out in significant detail.

Accordingly, it is in the work of the psychologist Hugo Münsterberg where Weber finds 'the most systematic development of the fundamental theses of [that] philosophy of science' according to which the 'subjectifying' (as opposed to the 'objectifying') sciences study a special kind of *being (Sein) (R & K,* p. 130) which is 'a wholly different sort of reality' (Münsterberg 1900, p. 51). This 'being' is none other than Brentano's (and Wundt's and Dilthey's) 'psychical' or 'mental' domain of inner experience. Conceived as that 'intentional' domain in Brentano's sense, i.e., that of *judging, evaluating, desiring, willing,* and so on, this notion is, as suggested above, the source of that conception of *Being* which emerges with fullness in Heidegger's *Being and Time* (1962 [1927]), a connection shown by Gilbert Ryle (1971, vol. 1, Chap. 12).

According to Weber's account, Münsterberg avers that we must separate the *nomological* sciences from the *subjectifying* sciences, for these latter:

have as their object a variety of *being (Sein)* which is in principle different from the objects of all those sciences like physics, chemistry, biology, and psychology... [*R & K*, p. 130.]

Moreover, this form of *being* is one 'which we immediately "experience" inwardly, but to which the notion of "psychical" as used in psychology does not apply' (my translation). If this claim were accepted, Weber continues, then it would provide us with a fundamentally different foundation for another kind of knowledge, one which rests on 'interpretation'.

The reader should note, however, that the translation of this section of Weber's text (*R & K*, p. 130; 1922, p. 71) is misleading. Weber is obviously discussing Section I, Chapter 2, of Münsterberg's *Fundamental Elements of Psychology* (1900, pp. 45-55), whose title is 'pure experience'. It is here that he talks about the 'ego' as an 'immediately experienced' actuality (or reality) which must always remain as such: it can *only* be 'directly experienced'. The translator has therefore mistranslated the phrase 'which we immediately "experience", inwardly', when he renders it as 'logically altogether different from the existence of that sort of concrete reality which is the object of *immediate* "experience"...' (*R & K*, p. 130).[5]

In any event, Weber suggests that this conception of 'interpretation' has not been carefully analyzed. Moreover, Münsterberg's book 'seems to present the concept of the irrationality of the "personal" in an altogether different sense' (p. 131). Consequently, the next fifty or so pages of *R & K* are devoted to the many versions of this thesis which proclaims a unique constitution of the experiences and expressions of mankind, thereby necessitating special methods of study. The parade of those who offer versions of this thesis include Friedrich von Gottl-Ottlilienfeld, Georg Simmel, Theodore Lipps, and Benedetto Croce. Whether or not Simmel rightfully belonged in this camp, Weber does in fact lump him together with the others.

It seems, then, that by 1905 Weber was particularly keen to combat 'all those errors' (especially those committed by Gottl), which 'have their source in every sort of psychologism, a confusion between the psychological processes reponsible for the origins of objective knowledge and the concepts in which this knowledge is *articulated*' (*R & K*, p. 257; original emphasis). Following Weber through this thicket of conceptions is no easy matter, and it is not surprising, as Marianne Weber later reported, that this 'essay of sighs' (p. 278) of *Roscher and Knies* 'soon turned into a burden and a torment' (1975, p. 260).

While Dilthey's work has a shadowy existence behind all of these writers, Weber credits Münsterberg's book and its views with having an 'immediate' impact on 'the theory of the "cultural sciences"' (p. 130). Furthermore, Münsterberg had linked Brentano, Dilthey, and even William James to his effort to begin inquiry in the 'subjectifying' sciences with the notion of the 'unity of consciousness' and a sharp separation of the 'physical' from the 'psychical' (Münsterberg 1900, Chap. 1). Thus, out of this movement there developed a stark dichotomy between the sciences. As set out by Münsterberg, history, historical economics and related fields are the subjectifying disciplines which are *logically* (and sometimes, *ontologically*) separated by subject matter and method from the natural sciences.

Gottl, on the other hand, presents the thesis of the complete certainty of 'immediate experience', while Lipps and Croce extend this through the joint

---

5 This passage (Weber 1922, p. 71) is an *exceedingly* difficult one to translate and it remains to be seen whether or not a satisfactory rendering of it can be reached on which any two scholars would agree. But a key to this and related passages is Münsterberg's concept of '*stellungnehmende Akualität*', or 'inner subjective commitment', which involves 'willing and judging' (Weber 1922, p. 94; Münsterberg 1900, pp. 50-51).

claim of a unique form of *inference* in the social sciences, achieved either through 'intuition' or a most fascinating complete *empathic* penetration into the minds of others. In Weber's view, however, Gottl rightly saw the 'inferential' nature of historical knowledge, and saw that the interpretative process (in Weber's restatement of Gottl's position):

proceeds by incorporating newly interpreted components of concrete reality into the interpretation. Inferences are made continually from the 'interpretation' of available 'sources' to the *meaning* of those actions for which these sources constitute the evidence. [*R & K*, p. 155.]

The problem was that Gottl thought this was qualitatively different from what takes place in the natural sciences. At the same time, he thought that in the historical sciences, because of the 'immediacy of experience', a greater certainty could be attained. Although Weber severely taxes Gottl's epistemological position, he nevertheless repeatedly stresses (in footnotes) the importance of Gottl's insights. In short, while Weber does not attempt to present his thoughts and criticism in a neat and tidy fashion, there is an inner coherence: by the time he finishes discussing Lipps and Croce, he has decisively defeated all the uniqueness claims of the authors discussed.

When Weber takes up Münsterberg's notion of 'being', he suggests that if we take it seriously, then rational action becomes impossible. This new realm of being contains the activities of the 'ego', and the ego is continuously involved in acts of willing, judging, and evaluating. But it seems to 'evaporate', without leaving any trace for us to analyze; therefore, for Münsterberg it is 'indescribable'. It is approachable only in the world of 'immediate experience'. If we take this literally, Weber notices,

then it is . . . obvious that rational reflection upon both the means required to achieve the purpose of a concrete 'action' and the possible consequences of the contemplated act would have no place in the world of unobjectified 'experience'. In every such reflection, the world *becomes* an 'object', a 'complex of observed facts' which falls under the category of causality. Without 'empirical' *generalizations* about the course of events— generalizations which can be produced only by 'objectifying' pure 'perception'—'rational' conduct is impossible. [P. 131f.; original emphasis.]

Nevertheless, the claim is made that the special instruments, or

the categories peculiar to 'subjectifying' knowledge are 'empathy' [*Einfühlen*] and 'understanding' [*Verstehen*]. They apply only within the domain of 'mental processes' [and] there are no rules of correspondence which connect these categories to the instruments of objectifying knowledge. [P. 135.]

We see, then, that the writings of Münsterberg and Gottl (but also Lipps and Croce) are variations on this theme of the special 'empathic' method of 'knowing' in the social sciences. Accordingly, Weber fastens his attention on the 'decisive question' throughout this long encounter. Characteristically, Weber first formulates this decisive question at the end of a four page footnote which summarizes Münsterberg's 'logical defects'. There he puts the question:

If history is a 'system of intentions and purposes' [Münsterberg's phrase, 1900, p. 14], then the really decisive question is the following. Is there a variety of 'understanding' [*Verstehen*] which is 'objective' in the sense that it does not evaluate its subject matter by 'taking a position', but only attempts to establish 'valid' conclusions concerning the actual properties and relations of 'matters of fact'? [P. 246.]

Weber's answer to this would seem to be in the affirmative, since he had earlier shown that in the natural sciences 'interpretations' are also produced. However, the epistemological issues are stated differently here in the writings of Münsterberg, Gottl and the others so as to suggest that the subject matter of the sociocultural sciences is suspended in an *ontological* space in which wholly different epistemological principles prevail. Consequently, Weber persists in the task of analyzing and defusing each of the alternative arguments for the epistemological uniqueness of the 'subjectivity' of social 'being'.

In response to Münsterberg's notion that history must be a 'subjectifying' science set off from the nomological sciences, Weber states the obvious in his typically perspicuous fashion. 'The decisive point is', he writes,

[that] history is simply not confined to the domain of 'mental life'. On the contrary, it 'conceives' the entire historical constellation of the 'external' world as both motive and as a product of the 'mental life' of the bearers of historical action. That is to say: things which, in their concrete multiplicity, have no place in a psychological laboratory. [P. 136.]

On the other hand, Weber sees no reason why results obtained by 'objectifying' sciences could not be brought to bear upon problems in history. For example, 'it is not at all clear why . . . the exact psychological analysis of religious hysteria *could* not establish results which history could use and would be obliged to use as auxiliary concepts for the causal explanation of specific concrete processes' (p. 137). This is not the same as arguing that some set of psychological 'laws of thought' must be the basis of history and the human sciences. It is rather the different claim that if certain psychological mechanisms were discovered, and their domain of applicability were reasonably well known, then history could indeed learn from, let us say, psychopathology. '*Whenever* this is done', Weber argues,

e.g., whenever history learns from pathology that certain 'actions' of Friedrich Wilhelm IV fall under certain verified generalizations concerning psychopathic reactions—then the result is precisely what Münsterberg regards as impossible: an 'objectifying' explanation is produced for 'items which are not understood'. [P. 137; original emphasis.]

In other words, from the point of view of 'rational calculation' and typical conduct, certain actions of the Kaiser may appear to be 'incomprehensible'. Yet those very actions would make sense—would fall into an explanatory pattern—if certain psychological processes or mechanisms were known to exist. Thus 'objectified' knowledge about human subjects serves to elucidate and explain what is *not* 'empathically' comprehended or 'understood'.

Moreover, Weber goes forward to suggest that

we shall see that 'interpretation' need not be *restricted* to an account of concrete processes. Investigations in 'social psychology', insofar as they exist at present, for the most part employ the tools and the aims of interpretation [*Deutung*]. But their results are 'nomothetic' *generalizations*. [P. 246, n. 31; original emphasis.]

In short, Weber *repeatedly* stresses that 'interpretation' is a necessary activity in all domains of scientific inquiry: in the so-called 'subjectifying' sciences as well as the 'objectifying' sciences; in the 'nomothetic' disciplines as well as the 'individualizing' sciences.[6] Several pages later Weber uses the example of 'animal psychology' to point out that it 'also employs "interpretations"', and as 'regards their original content, the 'teleological' components of biological concepts also include "interpretations"' (p. 151).

Thus even granting that 'the invariable criterion of the "subjectifying" sciences', as *historical* disciplines, 'is "empathy", "reproduction in immediate experience", in short, "interpretive understanding"', we may suppose

that the disciplines which attempt to achieve this sort of understanding also attempt to produce a *scientific* account of the facts. It is one of the essential features of such an account that it aims at intersubjectively *valid* 'objective truth'. In which case, the concrete mental process that is the object of interpretive understanding, for example, 'volition' that is 'immediately' understandable and the 'ego' in its 'immediately' understandable 'unity' can never escape objectification. [P. 148.]

Accordingly, Weber finds it necessary to introduce a distinction between two or more ambiguous meanings of the concept 'interpretation' [*Deutung*]:

(1) It can be an allusion to a specific emotional *commitment*—for example, the 'suggestiveness' of a work of art or a 'beauty of nature'. In this case, 'interpretation' denotes the imputation of a '*valuation*' of a specific quality.

Under this heading one may place those 'interpretations' which are designed to grasp some spiritual or ontological message. Or:

(2) 'interpretation' can be the imputation of a judgment, in the sense of an affirmation that an *actual* set of relations is validly 'understood'. This is the only sort of 'interpretation' [*Deutung*] we are discussing here, the sort of 'interpretation' which produces knowledge of *causal* relations. It is impossible to interpret the 'beauty of nature' in this sense unless one makes metaphysical claims. [P. 149; original emphasis.]

Here again Weber links 'interpretation' with the supplying of 'causal knowledge', but not in a positivist sense. Although historical inquiry begins with *value relations* (and in that sense one may grant that 'to a certain extent evaluative interpretation is the inevitable precursor of causal interpretation' [p. 149]), in all cases of interpretation of historical persons and events,

use of the categories in which concrete reality is conceived as 'directly experienced' [*erlebten*] and 'reproduced in direct experience' [*nacherleben*] *serves the purpose* of 'objectifying' knowledge. [P. 151; original emphasis.]

With these assumptions, Weber approaches an issue of great importance and one which all of Weber's interpreters routinely overlook. For example, the author of one of the most recent major studies of Weber's methodological writings seems to think that Weber has a 'theory of understanding as reex-

---

6 The claim that Weber 'calls "interpretation" an "absolutely secondary category which has its home in the artificial world of science"' (Burger 1976, p. 195) is an extreme misunderstanding of Weber's position, no doubt a failure here to realize that this *would be* the consequence of Münsterberg's argument, not Weber's. Burger's reference is to a passage where Weber is discussing Münsterberg's views (and where he contrasts it to Simmel's; *R & K*, p. 153; 1922, p. 94).

periencing' and that 'as far as it can be extrapolated and reconstructed from his dispersed remarks—of course has many loose ends' (Burger 1976, p. 110f.).

But the epistemological point surely is that it is one thing to 'experience' something, yet it is quite another to know *what* it is that has been experienced. Both Rickert (1962, p. 65) and Weber saw that pure 'experience' is not science. Hence, in response to Gottl's views (i.e., in *Der Herrschaft des Wortes*, 1901), Weber insisted that

even within the domain of the personal, a 'concept' is invariably different from the 'experience' on which it rests, regardless of whether the concept is a mental construct developed by generalized abstraction or by isolation and synthesis. [P. 255, n. 54.]

Here again Weber combats the confusion between psychological 'experience' and 'knowledge'.

Moreover, it should be obvious that this whole orientation to the *immediacy* of 'inner perception' is but a variant of the sensationalist epistemological thesis according to which sensations are the immediate source of all knowledge, the source from which knowledge is *directly derived*. Furthermore, in the case of both Gottl and Münsterberg (as we have noted), there is an additional element of absolute certainty added to this sensationalism.

Discussing Gottl's book, Weber writes, 'The claim has been made—and Gottl is in basic agreement with it—that "our own immediate experience" is the most certain piece of knowledge that we have' (p. 160). In a footnote, Weber adds, '[l]ike so many others, Münsterberg . . . shares this opinion too. The "nonmechanical meaning" of the "act" of another "subject" is immediately given' (p. 261, n. 60). Consequently, it would seem to be a direct reference to the phenomenological tradition of Brentano, whose formulation of this sensationalist view we have already discussed, for Weber to use the locution, 'the claim has been made'.

To this assertion Weber replies:

The claim that every 'experience' [*Erlebnis*] is perfectly certain obviously shows *that* we experience. However, *what* we really experience can become accessible to 'interpretation' only after the 'experience' itself has lapsed. In which case, what is experienced can become the 'object' of a proposition. The content of this proposition is no longer 'experienced' in inchoate stupor. On the contrary, it is recognized as 'valid'. [P. 162.]

Clearly Weber does not share the perspective according to which we 'experience truth', nor would Weber use the phrase of the contemporary hermeneutic tradition in which one talks of 'that experience of truth that transcends the sphere of the control of scientific method' (Gadamer 1975, p. xii).

But neither is Weber adopting an allegedly 'positivist' stand. On the contrary Weber was, in contemporary jargon, a 'post-empiricist' long ago when the logical positivists were only beginning their ill-fated enterprise. Weber recognized that in *both* natural science and history 'guess work' and 'intuition' are of critical significance:

The role which our 'historical'—or more generally, interpretive—imagination plays in the 'inference' of historical processes is no different from its role in the domain of physical knowledge. Consider, for example, the role of the 'mathematical imagination'. The testing of hypotheses discovered in this fashion—for hypotheses are employed in both domains— is from a logical point of view . . . the same in both domains. [P. 156.]

The same view and comparison involving Ranke is repeated in the 'Critical Studies' essay of 1906 where Weber refers to Ranke's 'divining' of the past. 'But it is absolutely no different with the really great advances in knowledge in mathematics and the natural sciences. They all arise intuitively in the flashes of imagination as hypotheses. . .' (1949, p. 176). Thus while Weber insisted that 'interpretative understanding' always involves 'objectification' and the formulation of concepts, he simultaneously maintained that the difference between the social and natural sciences 'does not lie in the function of "inference"', which Gottl, for example, tried to maintain (p. 156ff.).

Moreover, Weber was willing to grant a considerable role to the use of analogies in the interpretation of human action, especially in the process of self-understanding.

It is not the exception, but the rule, that interpretation proceeds by the use of *analogies* [*Analogie*]. That is, by introducing the 'experience' of *others* which are intentionally *selected* for the purpose of comparison. Therefore, an unconditional presupposition of 'interpretation' is a certain amount of conceptual isolation [*Mass von Isolation*] and analysis. This is not only a necessary condition for 'interpretation'. 'Interpretation' *must* be analyzed and verified in this way in order to have the properties of clarity and precision which Gottl ascribes to it *a priori*. The leaden diffuseness of 'immediate experience' [*Erlebens*] must be broken. . . in order to take even the first step toward a genuine 'understanding' [*Verstehen*] of *ourselves*. [P. 162; 1922, p. 104; original emphasis.]

We may, therefore, return to Weber's strategic insight that the processes of *Einfühlen* ('empathy') and *Nacherleben* ('reliving') 'serve the purpose of "objectifying" knowledge' (original emphasis). For '[t]his point has consequences which are methodologically both interesting and important. But they are not the consequences that Münsterberg supposes', for the question of what exactly those consequences are 'can be answered only by a *theory of interpretation*, a theory which at this point is barely visible and has hardly been explored at all' (p. 151; original emphasis).

In saying this, Weber found no aid or solace in the writings on 'hermeneutics' of his day. 'The work of Schliermacher and Boeckh on "hermenuetics" ', Weber adds precipitously in a footnote, 'are not relevant here, since they do not pursue epistemological aims'. Furthermore, Weber notes, Dilthey's account, contained in his 'Ideas on a Descriptive and Analytic Psychology',

and decisively rejected by the psychologists (Ebbinghaus) is weakened by the following prejudice: the belief that specific systematic *sciences* must correspond to certain formal categories of our knowledge. [P. 250, n. 46.]

Likewise Weber was aware of Dilthey's other writings, especially Dilthey's paper 'On the Development of Hermeneutics' (1900, now in Rickman pp. 246-63).

In sum, Weber found the writings of the turn-of-the century on 'understanding' and 'interpretation' to fall short of the mark regarding adequacy. Secondly, he perceived that discussions of the problems of understanding and interpretation fall within the domain of epistemology, and that few writers seemed to be cognizant of the need for a *theory* of interpretation. It may be conceded that Weber did not explicitly work out such a theory (nor did he claim to have done so). Instead, in the next sections of *R & K*, he avows the intention of attempting 'only to establish the status and possible importance of the problem *as I see it*' (original emphasis). With such matters in mind, we may turn to Weber's analysis of Georg Simmel's methodological views concerning the processes of 'understanding' and 'interpretation'.

REFERENCES

Ayer, A. J. (1964) *Man as a Subject for Science*. Oxford.

Bacon, Francis (1960) *The New Organon*. Indianapolis.

Bruun, H. H. (1972) *Science, Values, and Politics in Max Weber's Methodology*. Copenhagen.

Burger, Thomas (1976) *Max Weber's Theory of Concept Formation*. Durham.

Davidson, Donald (1968) 'Actions, Reasons, and Causes', in May Brodbeck (ed.), *Readings in the Philosophy of the Social Sciences*. New York, pp. 44-58.

Dilthey, Wilhelm (1977) *Descriptive Psychology and Historical Understanding*. The Hague.

Drake, Stillman (ed.) (1957) *Discoveries and Opinions of Galileo*. New York.

Feyerabend, Paul (1962) 'Explanation, Reduction, Empiricism', in H. Feigl and G. Maxwell (eds.), *Minnesota Studies in the Philosophy of Science*, vol. 3. Minneapolis, pp. 28-97.

Gadamer, Hans-Georg (1976) *Truth and Method*. New York.

Gottl, Friedrich (1901) *Der Herrschaft des Wortes*. Jena.

Hart, H. L. A. and A. M. Honoré (1959) *Causation in the Law*. Oxford.

Heidegger, Martin (1962) *Being and Time*. London.

Mill, John Stuart (1965) *On the Logic of the Moral Sciences*. Indianapolis.

Münsterberg, Hugo (1900) *Grundzüge der Psychologie*. Leipzig.

Nelson, Benjamin (1975) 'The Quest for Certitude and the Books of Scripture, Nature, and Conscience', in O. Gingerich (ed.), *The Nature of Scientific Discovery*. Washington, pp. 355-73.

Peirce, C. S. (1931-35) *Collected Papers*, 6 vols. Cambridge.

Popper, Karl (1974) *Objective Knowledge*. New York.

Reichenbach, Hans (1938) *Experience and Prediction*. Chicago.

Rickert, Heinrich (1962) *Science and History*. New York.

Rickman, H. P. (ed. and trans.) (1976) *W. Dilthey. Selected Writings*. Cambridge.

von Schelting, Alexander (1934) *Max Webers Wissenschaftslehre*. Tübingen.

Weber, Marianne (1975) *Max Weber. A Biography*. New York.

Weber, Max (1922) *Gesammelte Aufsätze zur Wissenschaftslehre*. Tübingen.

———— (1949) *The Methodology of the Social Sciences*. New York.

———— (1968) *Economy and Society*. Totowa.

Whewell, William (1840) *The Philosophy of the Inductive Sciences*, 2 vols. London.

CHAPTER THREE

Simmel's 'essay', *The Problems of the Philosophy of History* (1977), was first published in 1892. The second and completely revised version (according to Simmel's own testimony) appeared in 1905, and is the basis of the present translation by Guy Oakes. And Oakes has supplied us (Note 15, p. 35 of his 'Introduction') with indications of the sections which were newly added to the second edition, or which were extensively rewritten.

The intent of this work, Simmel reports in the Preface to the second edition, is to provide a critique of 'historical realism: the view according to which historical science is simply a mirror image of the event "as it really happened"' (p. vii). In other places, Simmel states his critique in the form of asserting that:

Even in the most obvious cases, it is not 'the plain fact' that resolves the question of the intelligibility of the consequences of a phenomenon. On the contrary, psychological premises—in relation to which 'the plain fact' serves as a major premise—are responsible for the fact that the consequence of a phenomenon seems to be possible and intelligible. We subsume observable human actions under the observable purposes and feelings which are necessary in order to fit these actions into an intelligible scheme. [Pp. 50-51.]

But, as we see here, Simmel also hoped to establish what he called (adopting Kantian language), 'the *a priori* of historical knowledge' (p. viii). Throughout the essay Simmel takes for granted that the existence of 'psychological states', 'mental states', and the like serve as 'the basis' for historical inference. True to form, Simmel raises a host of fascinating questions about the nature and possibility of historical knowledge, yet the composite result is much closer to a string of pearls—by no means of uniform colour, significance, or shape—than a consistent set of notions. One can find in Simmel's pages a large number of insights which seem to be anticipations of Weber's views. Yet on nearly every occasion of this sort, one finds Simmel arguing the *opposite* position either on the next page or shortly thereafter.

For example, Simmel writes:

It is obvious that law and morals, language and thought, high culture and forms of social intercourse do not develop independent of the *intentional* activities of individuals. [P. 54; my emphasis.]

Thus it would seem that historical developments are to be explained by reference to actors' motives, purposes and intentions. But,

Consider the theory of the forces of economic production, forces which either mesh with existing forms of production or outgrow and destroy them. . . . Consider, for example, the transition from slavery to the feudal system and the transformation of feudalism into an economy of wage labor. Suppose that wage labor also 'evolves' into socialism. The explanatory causes of these transformations cannot be found in the consciousness of the actors themselves. On the contrary, they lie—as this might be expressed—in the logical consequences of the existing economic technology, the productive forces it generates and the constitution of the society in which these forces are expressed with mechanical necessity. Consciousness, therefore, is completely irrelevant to the identification of these explanatory causes. [P. 55.]

Thus we are faced with a conundrum: if 'socialism' is a 'higher form' of cultural development, how could it develop without the existence of 'intentional activity' on the part of actors, even if that intentional activity did not clearly strive to achieve 'socialism'? If we are to frame an explanation of this outcome, are we to subscribe to the blind 'laws of history' (or 'technology'), or do we require some explanatory reference to the *intentions* and *purposes* of actors? Simmel seems to have it both ways.

Despite the existence of logical inconsistencies of this sort which abound in *The Problems of the Philosophy of History* (*PPH* hereafter), Weber credits Simmel with

the elucidation of the most extensive range of cases which fall under the concept of 'understanding'—'understanding', that is, in contrast to 'discursive knowledge' of reality which is not given in 'inner' experience. [*R & K*, p. 152.]

On the other hand, Weber's praise of Simmel is frequently belied by Weber's great facility in using seemingly ready-made conceptions in quite the opposite sense of their original creators.

For example, Weber lauds Simmel when he points out that Simmel

has clearly distinguished the objective 'understanding' of the *meaning* of an expression from the subjective 'interpretation' of the *motive* of a (speaking or acting) person. In the first case, speech is the object of 'understanding', in the second case, the speaker (or agent). [*R & K*, p. 152.]

However, when Simmel contrasted the understanding of the *objective import* of an utterance with the case in which the 'subjective intention' of the actor is used to interpret the utterance, he used the term 'motive' in an inherently psychological fashion. His 'motives' are 'prejudice, anger, anxiety, or sarcasm'.

Suppose we identify this *motive* for the expression or utterance. In this case, the sense in which we 'understand' the utterance is very different from the sense in which we grasp its import. In this case, understanding is not only concerned with comprehension of what is spoken, it is also concerned with comprehension of the act of speaking. [*PPH*, pp. 54-55.]

Thus, (*a*) Simmel's 'motives' seem to be 'psychological' states of 'feeling', whereas Weber uses the idea of motive to refer to 'a complex of subjective meaning which seems to the actor himself or the observer an adequate ground for the conduct in question' (1968, p. 11). Moreover, (*b*) Weber's 'rational interpretation' in terms of *motives* is 'not concerned with a "psychological" analysis of "personality"...' (*R & K*, p. 188). Consequently, Weber refers to the deciphering of motives as a means of arriving at the 'meaning' of *both* 'everyday' and 'objective' (or theoretical) utterances. Simmel in contrast, had separated the case of theoretical understanding from that of other cases. Additionally we should note that Simmel describes the process of understanding in terms of psychological states and the re-experiencing of 'mental states'. According to Simmel,

> We must be able to recreate the mental act of the historical person. As this is sometimes expressed, we must be able to 'occupy or inhabit the mind of the other person'. The understanding of an utterance entails that the mental processes of the speaker—processes which the words of the utterance express—are also reproduced in the listener by means of the utterance. [*PPH*, p. 64.]

To this Weber naturally responds: 'I doubt that this psychological description of the *logical* character of *this* sort of "understanding" is sufficiently precise' (*R & K*, p. 153; original emphasis). Furthermore,

> The decisive point is as follows: all these cases of 'understanding'—'understanding' of an order, a question, a claim, an appeal to sympathy, etc.—are concerned with a process which takes place within the sphere of 'inner subjective commitment'.[7] [Pp. 154-55.]

Let us consider the case of the military patrol officer who

> receives a written command which is ambiguously-drawn up. It is necessary for him to 'interpret' the 'purpose' of the order—that is to say, to consider the motives responsible for the order—in order to act on it. The *causal* question, 'What is responsible for the 'psychological' genesis of the order?' is, therefore raised in order to answer the 'noetic question' concerning its 'meaning'. In this case, the theoretical 'interpretation' of personal action, and ultimately of the personality (of the person giving the order), is employed in the service of [immediate], practical purposes. [P. 154; original emphasis.]

In short, the presentation of a military order is accompanied by a lack of understanding of the order's *meaning*. In order to grasp that meaning, resort must be had to the *reasons* or *motives* for the order's issuance in the first place. The reasons for the order's issuance in the first place would make clear the 'purpose' (*Zweck*) of the order and that would reveal to the junior officer what

---

7 The phrase, 'inner subjective commitment', is my rendering of '*stellungnehmenden Aktualität*'. Oakes translated it (understandably) as 'the sphere of the "commitments of everyday life"' (*R & K*, p. 154; Weber 1922, p. 94). Weber has borrowed the term from Münsterberg's discussion of 'pure experience' and the 'ego'. According to Münsterberg, the 'ego' *can only* be directly experienced and therefore it remains an 'inner subjective commitment' (*stellungnehmende Aktualität*; 1900, p. 50). However it makes no sense in Weber's text to translate the latter term as 'quotidian'—an error which Oakes regrettably reifies in his 'Introductory Essay' to the *Critique of Stammler* (p. 50 n15). There he refers to '"*aktuelles Verstehen*" or "quotidian understanding"', and refers the reader to the passage in *Roscher and Knies* in question here. But '*aktuelles Verstehen*' is not 'quotidian understanding'—whatever that might be—but refers to Münsterberg's *phenomenological* interpretation which is 'immediately experienced', and which is allegedly 'non-conceptual', a logical impossibility it would seem. But there is still another complication, for when the term appeared later in *Economy and Society*, Talcott Parsons was led to translate it as 'direct observational understanding' (see Weber 1968, p. 8 and n7, p. 58). No doubt Weber changed the meaning of the term again, but when such a translation yields the locution, '*rational* observational understanding' (p. 8; my emphasis), I think we may conclude that something has gone awry.

the full meaning of the order was. What the recipient of the command needs to know is some sort of description of the military situation which the commanding officer faced, and which therefore, prompted him to write the order. Such a description would involve an assessment of 'typical' military strategy and procedure, typical purposes, and hence typical reasons and responses, i.e., 'motives' and 'intentions'. Accordingly, Weber suggests that the 'meaning' of an act or utterance is tied to an 'intentional' complex of typical modes of evaluating and responding. It is not a 'psychological' problem of 'recreating' the 'mental states'

or 'contents' of the officer's mind. It is rather 'an "inference" of the meaning of an action which presupposes the *rational* character of the motivation of the action. Such an inference is invariably only a hypothesis proposed for the purpose of "interpretation"' (pp. 158-59). Moreover, the '"normal" man and "normal" action are obviously just as much ideal-typical conceptual constructs developed for certain purposes as—in the reverse sense—the famous "sick horse" in Hoffman's *The Iron Knight*' (p. 159).

Nevertheless, Simmel, even in the third (1907) edition of *PPH* persisted with his psychological view: 'The issue', he wrote, 'is not an epistemological problem, but rather a psychological problem within epistemology' (*PPH*, p. 209, n8). Consequently, in his attempt to explain the workings of 'genius' in the interpretation of 'phenomena that do not lie within the domain of immediate experience', Simmel resuscitates the Platonic view according to which 'the genius's apparently super-empirical ability to recreate mental processes' is a result of

a process whereby one becomes conscious of an inheritance that is unconscious or latent. In some form or other, earlier generations have transmitted their organic modifications to later generations; in some obscure fashion, the organic modifications are related to mental processes. [*PPH*, p. 95.]

On this rather implausible 'biological version of the Platonic theory of anamnesis', Weber's comment is:

Such a theory would be unobjectionable even as a hypothesis only if every man numbered among his ancestors a person with the individual 'experiences' of Caesar, experiences which would be inherited in some way. [P. 258, n57.]

In short, Simmel failed to see that the 'meaning' of *any* utterance is inherently tied to an historically given set of typical motives, intentions and cultural cues, and that this way of framing the issues takes them out of the domain of 'psychology'.

Furthermore, Weber wrote in criticism of Gottl,

It is obvious that 'interpretation' cannot be conceived as the exclusive product of an intuition and a simple reproduction of experience which is independent of 'objectification'. First, the interpretive 'inference' of a concrete thought is occasionally based upon clinical-pathological knowledge. [P. 159.]

In such a case, the 'object' of understanding would already be described in 'theoretical' terms. But 'understanding' obviously would not in such a case require 'pathological feelings'.

At this point it may be best to set out a more schematic presentation of Weber's many criticisms of the 'empathic' method of 'interpretation' which rests on a peculiar conception of the irrationality of the human personality.

Throughout Weber's discussion of these issues, he lumped Simmel's views with those of Münsterberg and Gottl. It therefore appears that Weber considered Simmel's position to have much in common with theirs, and that an examination of the epistemological issues raised by Gottl for example, would allow us 'to either accept or reject Simmel's views' (*R & K*, p. 155). And it is at this point that Weber appends a footnote promising a systematic study of Simmel's work in the near future. But it was never to appear. However, the fragment of comments on Simmel recently published by Donald Levine (Weber 1972) would appear to be the beginning of that examination which soon broke off, never to be resumed.

In any event, the following assertions are the ones which Weber defends in the last part of his study. They may serve as amplification and clarification of the earlier criticisms directed at Münsterberg and Gottl, but now offered in criticism also of Lipps and Croce, and occasionally Simmel.

(1) There is no epistemological difference in the processes of 'understanding' and 'interpretation' for 'theoretical' and 'practical' purposes. Both contexts require guesses and speculations about meanings and motives; both use ideal-typical constructions in formulating 'interpretations' of social and natural events. That this is especially so in the domain of social life was illustrated by the example of the military order.

At the same time, Weber wished to restrict the notion of 'interpretation' to conscious reflection about the motivation for the act in question. I.e. (in response to Simmel)

Was there, for whatever reasons, *cognitive* reflection concerning this *motive* for the expression—even if the purposes of this reflection were practical? What we call 'interpretation' in this *paper* becomes applicable *only if* this condition is satisfied. [P. 154 n52; original emphasis.]

In other words, 'interpretations' of human acts involve inferences which rest upon the *assumption* of 'the rational character of the motivation of the action', and thus 'meaning' is directly tied to the 'rational' context which constitutes (what we may call) the 'reasons' or 'motives' for the action in the first place.

(2) '[It] is obviously a very serious mistake to claim knowledge of historical events is grounded in "logical laws of thought" when only the following is meant: historical events can be "interpreted"' (p. 158).

The point is that the alleged 'laws of thought' do not give us direct access to 'understanding'. It is rather a variety of *conceptual* notions (and guesses) about the way the world and a *particular* society operate which give us this access. Included within this armamentarium of access points are 'ideal typical' constructions and 'empirical generalizations', for example, about 'clinical' or 'pathological' behaviour. Earlier Weber used the case of Wilhelm IV and the possible use of psychological generalizations to interpret his behaviour (p. 137). Moreover, just these considerations suggest the 'theory-laden' character of both 'observation' and 'interpretation'. Consequently rejection of the *methodological* principle of the need for interpretation *because* of the existence (or nonexistence) of 'logical laws of thought' requires rejection of this vague methodological supposition, i.e., 'the proposition that "in principle" all men are "equal"' (p. 159). The 'normal' man is obviously an ideal construct. On the other hand, it is the instruments of concept formation, our theoretical hunches and so on, based on *historical* (or general) assumptions about 'human nature'—

and thus not 'intuition of pure being'—which makes 'interpretation' possible. However, variants of the 'laws of thought' or the ontological modes of 'experience' thesis require a further logical consideration:

(3) 'When one begins to think, *first person* experiences are replaced by reflection upon third-person experiences which are conceived as an "object". Only one sound point can be identified in this account [of "empathy" by Lipps]: as a matter of fact, "intellectual understanding" includes "inner participation",... "empathy". But insofar as its intention and goal is "knowledge", it is a "participation" in purposefully selected aspects' (p. 166).

Here Weber has decisively distinguished between 'knowledge' and 'experience' (or 'feeling'). In Weber's account of Lipps's theory of 'empathy', ' "empathy" is a propensity derived from "imitation": namely, the exclusively "inner" imitation of a process, for example the tightrope walk of an acrobat, as being "one's own"' (p. 164).

Weber rejects this as a methodological principle:

Whoever 'emphathizes' with Lipps's acrobat 'experiences' neither what the acrobat 'experiences' on the tightrope, nor what he would 'experience' if he were on the tightrope. What he 'experiences' does not even have any unambiguous, imaginative relationship to the experience of the acrobat. [Pp. 165-66.]

In addition to the logical point that there is a difference between 'knowledge' and 'experience', it may be pointed out that the acrobat, after all, will have had a long training period, a different early family life, etc., and consequently a very different mental set regarding walking on tightropes. It is not, in other words, the pure communality of 'minds'—and surely not the *identity* of 'experience'—that makes understanding of others (or ourselves) possible; it is rather the use of language, knowledge of cultural forms, the formulation of conceptual devices, and the discovery and use of various sorts of 'empirical generalizations'.

But Weber cannot bring himself to end these criticisms without adding still another corrective. This lies in the sharp distinction between 'self-evidence' (a term used by Brentano) and 'validity', as well as that between 'heuristic feeling' and 'valid' or 'causally essential' description. Therefore we must add the following logical point:

(4) 'this "self-evidence" of the object of interpretive "understanding" must be carefully distinguished from every relation germane to "logical validity". From a *logical* point of view, it presupposes only the *conceivability* of "interpretation". From a *substantive* point of view, it presupposes the objective possibility of "interpretation"' (p. 175f).

In other words, *logically* any interpretation is possible so long as it does not include logical absurdities or simple contradictions. The notion of 'pseudospherical space', Weber noted (following Helmholtz, *R & K*, p. 266, *n*76 [with which Cf. Helmholtz 1977, Chapter I]) does not involve a 'logical' impossibility or contradiction. On the other hand, from a factual point of view, an 'interpretation' needs only to be consistent with 'received' empirical knowledge. It must not, that is, imply processes, entities or *events*, that are strongly believed to contradict empirical findings.

We ought to stress here that Weber has implicity—and clearly in note 76— used an analogy based on Helmholtz's work on the axioms of geometry. This influence of Helmholtz is of considerable significance in the whole context of Weber's philosophy of science and conception of the 'logic of the cultural sciences'. But in connection with our topic here, Weber refers to Helmholtz's discussion of 'pseudospherical space' which implies a set of geometrical axioms of starkly *non*-Euclidean form. Such axioms might be said to be 'self-evident'. However, the point is that the question of whether or not these axioms— Euclidean or non-Euclidean—are an *actual* description of the world can only be determined through the conjoining of these axioms with *empirical* knowledge (and related assumptions) about perception, time, motion, and so on.

The decisive point in this section, however, is that there is an inevitable disjunction—Weber calls it a 'dualism'—in *all* fields of knowledge between the 'self-evidence' of concepts and hypotheses and 'the in fact world' (or strict *empirical* 'validity'); a dualism 'which obtains in the domain of the interpretation of human action [as well as] in the domain of those disciplines related to mathematics' (p. 175). A knowledge claim in any field must be evaluated both in terms of *logical* adequacy and in terms of 'empirical' adequacy: not in terms of simple 'self-evidence'.

These criticisms are directed in different ways toward Gottl, Simmel, and another writer by the name of Elsenhans. The animus of Weber's attack is clearly against the novel compound of the 'new empiricism' and the anti-naturalist school. The latter's attempt to substitute the criterion of 'self-evidence' was clearly a claim for special modes of cognition in the 'human studies'.

In the case of Gottl, Weber wrote,

the fundamental error of the theory of knowledge which Gottl accepts amounts to the following: it confuses the level of 'intuitive' self-evidence with the level of (empirical) *certainty*. The changing fate of the so-called 'axioms of physics' repeatedly illustrates the process. [P. 176; original emphasis.]

On the other hand, Simmel was as much an offender as Gottl regarding the notion of 'inner feeling', 'immediately given', as a criterion of 'validity'. Throughout *PPH*, Simmel consistently focusses on the *psychological* conditions of understanding, and insists on the point of view according to which 'the object of historical knowledge' is not just 'mind' but 'individuality'. Furthermore, this 'individuality' 'can only be psychologically comprehended or *grasped* by another person who has this same property of individuality' (p. 90; original emphasis). It might be noted that this assertion seems not to be compatible with the Simmelian phrase that 'one does not have to be Caesar in order to understand Caesar' (*PPH*, p. 94), and which Weber notes as a curious irony (*R & K*, p. 258 n57). But all of this appears to be of one piece with Simmel's theory of interpretation.

Thus when he discusses 'The Objectification of the Contents of Mental Processes' (*PPH*, pp. 68*ff*), Simmel in fact inserts a psychological 'feeling' as the only 'objective' criterion for establishing a particular interpretation. It is a 'feeling of psychological plausibility or appropriateness' (p. 69). While appearing to reject some criterion of 'Psychological nomological regularity' (p. 68), Simmel swings radically in the other direction of Gottl, Dilthey, Brentano and their followers. 'On the contrary', Simmel writes, 'the kind of general validity that is at stake here is a psychological property of mental activity itself. It is a feeling immediately given in mental activity' (p. 69). And it is this 'feeling' ('though it may not always decide with complete certainty in favor of *one'* construction) which 'provides the criterion which determines whether a mental construct that has a purely subjective origin is also objectively valid' (p. 69). In short, Simmel substitutes 'feeling' for objective and logical criteria of 'validity'.

Perhaps it is this theory which led Weber in 1920 to declare that his (Weber's) work, 'departs from Simmel's method (in his *Soziologie* and his *Philosophie des Geldes*) in drawing a sharp distinction between subjectively intended and objectively valid "meaning"; two different things which Simmel not only fails to distinguish but often deliberately treats as belonging together' (1968, p. 4). Of course, Weber had made this contrast public as early as 1913. In any event, Simmel proposed a purely psychological theory of understanding. In contrast, Weber wrote:

As regards the alleged 'certainty'—in the sense of scientific 'validity'—e.g., of 'feeling', every conscientious scholar must conclusively reject the following appeal: an appeal to 'feelings of totality'—e.g., to the 'general character' of an epoch, a work of art, etc.— which have not been translated into precisely articulated and demonstrable *propositions* which would verify them; that is, translated into 'conceptually' constituted 'observational experience'.]P. 178.]

Weber does not peremptorily reject 'feelings' out of hand; rather, he saw that

[t]he significance of 'feeling'—but note: a feeling acquired through constant *intellectual* occupation with the 'material', i.e., through practice and, therefore, 'observational experience'—for the psychological genesis of any hypothesis in the mind of an historian is certainly of eminent importance. [Pp. 177-78.]

What he opposed was an epistemological conclusion that it was the 'feeling' per se which was the source of validity, and the view that the 'feeling' was 'pure' and 'immediately experienced' independent of any conceptual awareness. And so on. In fine, mere 'self-evidence' is no more a criterion of validity in the social sciences than it is in mathematics or the natural sciences. One may conclude, therefore:

(5) 'As already shown, the role of "intuition", at least as regards its essential features, is the same in every domain of knowledge. Differences lie only in the *degree* to which an approximation to conceptual precision in discursive thought is possible and desirable' (p. 170).

With this we may conclude our review of Weber's unsurpassed probings of the epistemological foundations of 'understanding' and 'interpretation'. The details of Weber's discussions are far richer than what we have indicated here. And there are many additional issues which require both attention and careful study. But we may end our discussion of these aspects of *Roscher and Knies* with Weber's own summation:

Let us conclude this analysis—unavoidably somewhat monotonous—of the diverse theories of the alleged peculiarity of the 'subjectifying' disciplines and the significance of this peculiarity for history, theories which fairly glitter in the variety of their colors and forms. The only result of this analysis is really quite trivial. Nevertheless, its soundness has repeatedly been questioned. Consider any given piece of knowledge. Neither the 'substantive' qualities of its 'object' nor the 'ontological' peculiarities of the 'existence' of this 'object' nor, finally, the kind of *psychological* conditions required for its acquisition are of any consequence as regards its *logical* content and the presuppositions on which its 'validity' is based. *Empirical* knowledge in the domain of the 'mental' and in the domain of 'external' 'nature', knowledge of processes 'within' us and of those 'without' us is invariably tied to the instrument of 'concept formation'. From a logical point of view, the nature of a 'concept' in these two substantive 'domains' is the same. The *logical* peculiarity of *historical* knowledge in contrast to 'natural-scientific' knowledge—in the *logical* sense of this expression—has nothing at all to do with the distinction between the 'psychical' and the 'physical', the 'personality' and 'action', on the one hand, and the dead 'natural object' and the 'mechanical process of nature', on the other. To identify the 'self-evidence' of 'empathy' in the actual or potential 'conscious' inner 'experience'—an exclusively phenomenological sort of 'interpretation'—with a unique empirical 'certainty' of processes 'susceptible to interpretation' is an even more serious mistake. Physical and psychical 'reality', or an aspect of 'reality' comprehending both physical and psychical components, constitutes an 'historical entity' because and insofar as it can 'mean' something to us. 'Meaningfully' interpretable human conduct ('action') is identifiable by reference to 'valuations' and 'meanings'. For this reason, our criteria for *causal* explanation have a unique kind of satisfaction in the 'historical' explanation of such an entity. [Pp. 184-85.]

THE METHODOLOGY OF THE SOCIAL SCIENCES: CONCLUSION

A few words may be offered on the following heads: (*a*) Weber's notion of 'rational interpretation'; (*b*) the differences between Weber's 'intentional' frames of reference and those of Husserl and phenomenology; and (*c*) some convergences between Weber's approach and developments in 'ordinary language' philosophy and the 'hermeneutics' derived from *this* tradition.

(*a*) 'Rational interpretation' for Weber clearly implied, even in *R & K*, the supposition that 'we "understand" human action as determined by clearly conscious and intended "ends"' (p. 182). Naturally such a conception is an ideal typical device according to which behaviour might be assessed. It was, in other words, by virtue of supposing the 'means-end' schema that one could establish whether or not a particular course of action was 'rational'; i.e., whether or not the conduct was organized in the light of available knowledge and typical 'means' for realizing a general or specific end. Weber called the schema a 'teleological-*rational*' construct in *R & K*. An economic actor, for example, 'has the choice between economic destruction and the pursuit of very specific maxims of economic conduct' (p. 193). To the degree that the actor does deliberate about this course of action and does choose to follow these maxims, his behaviour is 'rational'. It is even 'purposefully *rational* conduct' (*zweckvoll-rationalen Handelns*; p. 194).

All of these goads to action, in Weber's terms, 'motives' for action, are (*a*) 'causes' of social action, and (*b*) *culturally* determined forms of responding to the 'world'. The 'purely rational constructs' of economics, Weber wrote, 'are possible only given the background of the concept of a money economy', and 'they do *not* contain *a single grain* of "psychology"' (p. 277 n96; original emphasis). In short, Weber's actors are located in a world of *culturally* shaped forms of existence and their linguistically and 'logically' shaped modes of thinking about, responding to, and interpreting the world.

Moreover, beginning in 1913 in his essay on 'Some Categories of Interpretive Sociology', Weber proceeded to recast his category of 'purposefully *rational* action' into a set of 'orientations' which could be geared to (1) 'rational expectations', (2) pure 'value' considerations (as in religious pursuits of salvation), and (3) emotional desires (1913, pp. 264ff; Graber 1970, pp. 62-64). In the last years of his life, Weber worked these alternative orientations to action into a typology which effectively constituted alternative modes of 'rationality'. These are the familiar types (set out in *Economy and Society*) of (1) 'instrumental rationality' (*zweckrationalität*), (2) 'value rationality' (*Wertrationalität*), (3) 'affectual' (or emotional) rationality, and (4) 'traditional rationality' (Weber 1968, pp. 24ff). Hence Weber took account of specifically *emotional* ('psychological') factors as well as 'traditional' forms of 'rationality' which diverge from what a 'scientific observer' might construe as 'objectively correct'. Furthermore, we have seen that Weber construed the elements of 'meaning' (which may be embodied either in underlying cultural values, grammatical rules, or rationally enacted *rules* of conduct [*Critique of Stammler*, pp. 94-143; Weber 1913, pp. 265ff. and Graber 1970, pp.64-78]) as *causes* of social action. In the methodological introduction to *Economy and Society*, Weber made explicit that 'a motive is a complex of subjective meaning which seems to the actor himself or to the observer an adequate ground for the conduct in question' (1968, p. 11). Therefore,

A correct causal interpretation of a concrete course of action is arrived at when the overt action and the motives have been correctly apprehended and at the same time their relation has become meaningfully comprehensible. A correct causal interpretation of typical action means that the process which is claimed to be typical is shown to be both adequately grasped on the level of meaning and at the same time the interpretation is to some degree causally adequate. [P. 12.]

From this point of view, that is, that of *causal* 'interpretation' (as first set out in *R & K*) the so-called 'operation called *Verstehen*' over which so much ink has been spilt, does not seem to be so mysterious and 'otherworldly' as many have supposed. Weber was concerned that there be a form of 'interpretation' in which there is 'an affirmation that an *actual* set of relations is validly "understood". This is the only sort of "interpretation" we are discussing here, the sort of "interpretation" which produces knowledge of *causal* relations' (*R & K*, p. 149; original emphasis).

Schematically, this account given by Weber for arriving at 'causal explanation' seems remarkably similar to Peirce's notion of 'abductive inference'. That is, given some puzzling (actions or) events, these events would make sense if they were part of a *hypothetical* constellation of processes characterized by properties *a, b, c*. If such hypothetical processes (and their properties) did obtain, then the puzzling (actions or) events would follow 'as a matter of course' (see Peirce 1931-35, vol. 5, p. 189; Hanson 1958, pp. 86ff.).

At the same time, Weber was insistent throughout *R & K* that there are no epistemological short cuts whereby one gains unmediated, direct, or infallible access to these explanatory processes and entities. Consequently, in *Economy and Society* Weber amplified this notion of explanation in terms of motives by postulating the need for confirmation (or corroboration) of such *hypothetical* explanations by 'established generalizations from experience [indicating that] there is a probability that it will always actually occur in the same way' (1968, p. 11). But Weber is not abandoning, as Winch (1958, pp. 111-16) seems to think, the explanatory pattern which attends to meanings and motives in favour of probabilistic or 'statistical' explanation. The underlying issue is not the contrast between 'meaningful' interpretation and probabilistic or 'statistical' explanation, but between 'self-evidence' and 'validity', the very same controversy that Weber explored in *R & K* (pp. 174ff). On this issue Winch overreacts, since Weber would agree that if a particular interpretation were incorrect, 'what is needed is a better interpretation, not something different in kind' (Winch 1958, p. 113).

Lastly, in this connection we may suggest that Weber's approach to the analysis of social action differs from Karl Popper's 'situational logic' (Popper 1962, vol. II, p. 97) in that Weber construed *motives* to be *causes* of social action, and that explanations framed in this manner do not rely on universal laws, but upon what might be called 'singular explanatory statements' (White 1965, Chapter 2; more on which below under [c]).[8]

(b) Given the above, therefore, there is the sharpest possible contrast between Weber's 'intentional' frames of reference and those of Brentano and Husserl, for both of whom there is no 'end' toward which particular acts are directed. 'Intentional acts' are simply states of 'awareness of something', an awareness of an 'object' of thought. Brentano's (and later, Husserl's) theory of intentionality *by design* (as we stressed earlier) has nothing to do with 'intentions' conceived as 'aims', 'ends', 'purposes', or 'motives'.

While Husserl went beyond Brentano in many respects, the notion of 'intentionality' remains within the domain of Brentano's non-scholastic view. Thus in his *Ideas for a Pure Phenomenology* (1931), Husserl speaks of 'intentional experiences' as those which 'are a consciousness of something' and to that degree 'they are said to be "intentionally related" to this something' (p. 119). And it should be obvious that *this* 'something' is *not* a set of motives or cultural orientations. For to arrive at the 'pure consciousness' of 'being', one must go by way of the 'phenomenological *epoché*', which means one must *suspend* the 'natural attitude', the beliefs, values, and cultural references of one's milieu.[9]

Moreover, Husserl challenged Brentano's notion of the 'inner certainty of experience' by transforming 'phenomenology' into 'the phenomenological inspection of essence', which is quaintly put as 'the turning of immanent ideation upon inner intuitions':

the turning of one's gaze on what is *proper* to the real (*reellen*) or intentional being of the experiences inspected, and only brings to an adequate focus the specific modes of experience which such individual experiences exemplify. [Husserl 1970 (1900), p. 607.]

---

8 The relationship between Weber's methodological position and that of Popper is far more intimate than has been supposed hitherto. Popper's 'logic of the situation' or 'situational logic' appears to me to be only a slightly modified version of Weber's 'rational interpretation' (cf. Weber in *R&K*, pp. 186-91, and Popper, 1957, pp. 149ff., and 141; as well as his 1962, vol. 2, p. 97). I hope to set out this comparison in greater detail in a forthcoming book.

9 I should state the difference between Husserlian and Weberian frames of reference as analogous to the difference between phenomenology and ordinary language philosophy. In the former, there is a withdrawal from 'everyday meanings' in order to arrive at 'essences', whereas in the latter, particularly in John Austin's hands, the study of *ordinary* language and its rules (especially the conventions of language use and dictionary reports) yield the 'meaning' of utterances and other forms of social action which is presumably embedded in cultural and linguistic conventions (see Austin 1962, and below under [c]). This contrast likewise applies to Schutz, whose 'in-order-to' and 'because-of-motives' (1967, pp. 86-96) are essentialist in nature and have no connection with the way ordinary ('everyday') users of a language think about their world.

Again, Husserl's 'intuited essences' are absolute universals: they were not thought to be shaped, coloured, determined, or whatever by 'mere' psychology, or more importantly, by *cultural* values. The 'mental acts' to be inspected by phenomenology are therefore 'pure acts of consciousness' uncontaminated by historical vagaries or cultural accretions. Husserl was prompted to reject Brentano's 'psychologism' out of fear, as Brentano put it in a letter of response to Husserl in 1905, that 'the laws of thinking which hold for us might be different from those that would hold of other thinking beings' (in Brentano 1966, p. 137).

In short, the animus of Husserl's thinking was precisely the desire to *escape* from culturally shaped forms of experience or 'modes of thought'. It therefore remains to be seen how such a procedure, how such a set of assumptions, can be said to be 'sociologically' relevant. Husserl's phenomenology deliberately blocked access to those peculiarly *historical* formations of cultural awareness which constitute the subject matter of sociological and anthropological investigation. Schutz's attempt to 'correct' Weber via Husserl and phenomenology is an historical irony whose progeny nevertheless inhabit sociological domains.[10]

Moreover, that form of 'hermeneutics' which traces its ancestry from Dilthey through Husserl to Heidegger is inherently incompatible with Weberian frames of reference for all of the reasons formulated by Weber in criticism of the phenomenological tradition from Brentano to early Husserl. Hermeneuticists who find their moorings in Husserlian intentionality are therefore operating within an epistemological and theoretical schema at odds with Weber's.

Finally, (c) we may consider some convergences of Weber's methodological thought with recent developments in philosophy and philosophy of language.

Until the early sixties the prevailing views regarding explanation in the social sciences seemed to be divided between those which insisted on the 'covering law model' and those which asserted that explanations of social action involve such notions as 'reasons', 'motives', 'purposes', and 'intentions', and that these latter are 'mentalistic' entities thereby precluding causal explanation. Yet Weber impressively argued that 'motives' as well as behavioural 'maxims', *and* 'rules of the game' serve as causes of social action. While the case for motives is stated in *R & K*, the case for 'maxims' and 'rules of the game' as causes are discussed in his *Critique of Stammler* (pp. 107-108, 113, 115). This little essay is the result of Weber's polemical study of Rudolf Stammler's book, *The Historical Materialist*

---

10 Although I must leave for another occasion a detailed discussion of Schutz's divergences from Weber's methodological (and epistemological) views, the recently published correspondence of the 1940s between the late Talcott Parsons and Alfred Schutz (see Grathoff, 1978) is a prime text which allows us to make the following 'retrodiction': Parsons and Schutz will be found there to differ most sharply where Parsons follows Weber's insights and Schutz follows the path of phenomenology. The fact that the differences between the two men stem from these contrasting philosophical and epistemological commitments has been overlooked by all three of the recent reviewers of the correspondence in *Contemporary Sociology* (**8**, 680-86). Furthermore, the difference between what an act 'means' 'objectively' to an observer and 'subjectively' to an actor (a distinction thought to be original to Schutz) is expressly spelled out by Weber in his *Critique of Stammler* (p. 112). See below in section [c]. Does this not raise the question of whether or not Schutz was a careful student of Weber's early methodological writings?

Conception of Economy and Law: A Sociophilosophical Investigation (1906).
But despite its polemical nature, Weber raised a lot of very important questions,
and formulated a number of very sharp and useful conceptions.

For example, in the *Critique* Weber points out that the 'meaning' of 'rules' of
conduct serve (in the language of John Searle [1969, pp. 33ff.] expanding
Wittgenstein) both as 'constitutive' and 'regulative' elements in social action.
Here is Weber's now classic example:

> Let us suppose that two men who otherwise engage in no 'social relation'—for example,
> two uncivilized men of different races, or a European who encounters a native in darkest
> Africa—meet and 'exchange' two objects. We are inclined to think that a mere description
> of what can be observed during this exchange—muscular movements and, if some words
> were 'spoken', the sounds which, so to say, constitute the 'matter' or 'material' of the
> behavior—would in no sense comprehend the 'essence' of what happens. This is quite
> correct. The 'essence' of what happens is constituted by the 'meaning' which the two
> parties ascribed to their observable behavior, a 'meaning' which 'regulates' the course of
> their future conduct. Without this 'meaning', we are inclined to say, an 'exchange' is
> neither empirically possible nor conceptually imaginable. Of course! The fact that 'ob-
> servable' signs function as symbols is one of the constitutive presuppositions of all 'social'
> relations. [*Critique*, p. 109.]

It is imperative to notice here, however, that in the next line Weber denies that
this property of having 'meaning' and 'symbolic' value is *peculiar* to 'social'
relations.

Another illustration of the contemporaneity of Weber's discussions in the
Critique is to be found in his assertion that "the 'rule' identifies a real 'cause' of . . .
actual conduct" (p. 107). In arguing for this, Weber is keen to point out that it is
not the rule itself which 'causes' the action, but rather the actor's subjective
intention to abide by the norm:

> For example, it is obviously not the conventional rule of greeting that tips my hat when I
> meet an acquaintance. On the contrary, my hand does it. But what is causally responsible
> for this? I may merely be in the 'habit' of following such a 'rule'. In addition, I may know
> from experience that my acquaintance would regard my failure to greet him as a lapse of
> propriety. The result would be unpleasant. In this case, therefore, the action is a conse-
> quence of a 'utilitarian' calculation. Or, finally, I may act on the belief that it is 'not proper'
> for me to disregard a harmless 'conventional rule' that is universally observed unless there
> is some compelling reason to do so. Therefore I act on the basis of my 'idea of a norm'.
> [*Critique*, p. 108.]

It is now recognized in the analysis of such examples (and in opposition to those
who assert that reasons and motives cannot be causes because their explanatory
use does not involve prior 'events'), that frequently there are two events which
might under some descriptions count as 'initial conditions' precipitating the
action. Thus in Weber's example, the 'precipitating' event might be found in the
appearance of Weber and his acquaintance in close proximity on the same street.
This in turn may prompt the 'noticing' of this event by Weber, and then the
tipping of his hat is caused by his decision to abide by the norm (convention) that
one should tip one's hat upon meeting an acquaintance of certain sorts. While we
may label the physical presence of the two men in close proximity as the 'initial
condition' triggering the action to be causally explained, it is clear that the mere
physical presence of the two men is not the 'cause' of the action, since it would
not have taken place if (*i*) the convention were nonexistent, or (*ii*) the other man

were a stranger, or (*iii*) Weber had decided not to act on the basis of the norm.

Likewise, in the case of 'the driver who signals a turn by raising his arm', Davidson argues, 'of course there is a mental event [preceding it]; at some moment the driver noticed (or thought he noticed) his turn coming up, and that is the moment he signaled' (1968, p. 52). But the defense of reasons as causes need not rest on the prior existence of an event, for two reasons. First, we may assume that there is a *constant flow* of action, rather than a disjointed set of actions. If we make this assumption, then it may be said that:

during any continuing activity, like driving, or elaborate performance, like swimming the Hellespont, there are more or less fixed purposes, standards, desires, and habits that give direction and form to the entire enterprise, and there is the continuing input of information about what we are doing, about changes in the environment, in terms of which we regulate and adjust our actions. To dignify a driver's awareness that the turn has come by calling it an experience, much less a feeling, is no doubt exaggerated, but whether it deserves a name or not, it had better be the reason why he raises his arm. [Davidson 1968, pp. 52ff.]

Put in a more theoretical language, under this description we may say that actions take place because of the existence of a 'battery of cultural cues' (Nelson 1981, Chapter 2) which have been internalized in individuals and thereby constitute 'states' and 'dispositions' to act in one way or another. Thus, secondly, as Morton White has put it,

it is false to say that an event can happen only because of an *event*. An automobile accident may have taken place because of the icy conditions of the road and, as we now see, this may be true without it following that where iciness can be predicted of a road on which automobiles are traveling, automobile accidents invariably follow. [1969, p. 254.]

Throughout Weber's methodological writings, he assumed that the subjective intentions of the actor are of paramount importance in explaining social action. Weber seems to have stressed this because he recognized that the 'meaning' of an action (or utterance) as perceived by an observer is always problematic and prone to be different from that of the actor. For example,

Consider the 'meaning' which 'we' could dogmatically or prescriptively ascribe to a process of this sort. Was it also the 'meaning' which each of the actual participants in this process consciously ascribed to it? Or did each of the participants ascribe some other 'meaning' to this process? Did they consciously ascribe any 'meaning' at all to the process? [*Critique*, p. 112.]

Thus while Weber clearly recognized the rule-following character of social action, he was keenly aware that interpreting the 'meaning' of the action was exceedingly complicated because of the intervention of subjective intentions. Thieves and card sharps Weber noted, might orient their conduct to the 'rules of the game' and the 'expectation' that normative patterns would be followed *for the purpose* of *deviating* from them (1913, pp. 269ff; Graber 1970, pp. 69-70).

Or in the case of our 'exchange' in darkest Africa,

the 'meaning' of the act of exchange might be the following. The actors consciously *intended to* impose an 'obligatory' *norm* upon their conduct. Therefore they had the (subjective) intention that their conduct should be obligatory because it should conform to this *norm*. In other words, they may have established a 'normative maxim'. On the other hand, the 'meaning' of the act of exchange might be the following. Each of the parties participates in the exchange in order to achieve a certain 'result'. In view of his 'experience', each sees his action as a 'means' for achieving this result. The exchange, therefore, has a (subjectively) intended 'purpose'. [*Critique*, p. 112.]

In short, there is an affinity between Weber's problematic and that which has become identified with the 'Oxford' philosophy of language school, as well as certain aspects of Wittgenstein's undertakings. If one chooses to call this a 'hermeneutic' tradition, then certainly it shares many of Weber's assumptions. Writers such as Paul Grice (1957) and Quentin Skinner (1972*a* and *b*) have sought to argue that the 'meaning' of (Austin's) illocutionary acts are decodable by reference to the actor's (or writer's) intentions. This, however, leaves open the question of the relationship between 'reasons' (as well as 'purposes') and 'intentions'. Davidson asserts that: 'To know a primary reason why someone acted as he did is to know an intention with which the action is done.... But to know the intention is not necessarily to know the primary reason in full detail' (1968, p. 48). Similarly, in his *Speech Acts*, Searle finds it necessary to reformulate Grice's claim that to recognize an actor's intention in uttering a remark is to understand the 'nonnatural' meaning of the act (see Searle 1969, pp. 43-58). Weber no doubt would have subscribed to the notions that (1) saying something is *doing* something (Austin 1962) and (2) that '*speaking a language* is engaging in rule-governed behavior' (Searle 1969, p. 41). Yet we are still left with the question, what is the theoretical relationship between 'reasons' (and 'motives'), 'purposes' (and 'intentions') and the larger *cultural context* in which they operate? To raise this latter question is to suggest that the supposition that reasons and intentions are integral to the explanation of social action (linguistic and non-linguistic alike) entails a *theory* of sociocultural process, a theory of the 'directive structures' of social life (cf. Nelson 1981, Chapter 2).

However all of this may turn out, it is now clear that Weber's methodological explorations at the turn-of-the-century are far from being exhausted regarding these issues. In their multiple thrusts they raise a great many questions about the nature and possibility of explanation in social science which continue to be of major concern today.

We owe a great debt to the translators of these works discussed above, especially Guy Oakes. In these methodological writings, written at the juncture of the twentieth century, virtually all of the logical problems which continue to inspire controversy and debate in the social sciences were given paradigmatic formulation.

What I have discussed here primarily as logical and epistemological issues regarding the logic of explanation in the social sciences should also be seen in relation to larger *metaphysical* positions. It should not escape the reader's attention that just as Weber raised severe doubts about Hegel's *metaphysical* position, Dilthey (and to a lesser degree Simmel) largely *accepted* and found inspiration in it. Likewise, while Weber was a committed Kantian, Husserl's (and Brentano's) moorings in the quest for certainty (see Kolakowski 1975) shaped by Descartes' pursuit of 'infallible methods' arrived at through the alleged suspension of cognitive categories, propelled him toward an 'essentialism' which is metaphysically opposed to Weber's Kantian metaphysics. The controversies reported in these essays seem so surprisingly familiar that we must surely ask ourselves, as Weber did in the case of Roscher, whether 'the logical weaknesses which lie concealed [within these writings] are in general clearer to us today than they were' to their authors.

REFERENCES

Austin, J. L. (1962) *How to Do Things with Words*. Oxford.

Brentano, Franz (1966) *The True and the Evident*. London.

Davidson, Donald (1968) 'Actions, Reasons, and Causes', in M. Brodbeck (ed.), *Readings in the Philosophy of the Social Sciences*. New York, pp. 44-58.

Graber, Edith E. (1970) 'A Translation of Max Weber's "Ueber Einige Kategorien Der Verstehenden Soziologie" . . . with Introduction and Footnotes'. Unpublished M.A. Thesis, University of Oklahoma.

Grathoff, Richard (ed.) (1978) *The Theory of Social Action: The Correspondence of Alfred Schutz and Talcott Parsons*. Bloomington.

Grice, Paul (1957) 'Meaning', *The Philosophical Review*, **66**, 377-88.

Hanson, N. R. (1958) *Patterns of Discovery*. Cambridge.

Helmholtz, Hermann (1977) *Epistemological Writings. The Paul Hertz/Moritz Schlick Centenary Edition of 1921*. Dordrecht.

Husserl, Edmund (1931) *Ideas. General Introduction to Pure Phenomenology*. London.

————— (1970) *Logical Investigations*, 2 vols. New York.

Kolakowski, L. (1975) *Husserl and the Search for Certitude*. New Haven.

Nelson, Benjamin (1981) *On the Roads to Modernity: Conscience, Science, and Civilizations*, ed. by T. E. Huff. Totowa.

Peirce, C. S. (1931-35) *Collected Papers* , 6 vols. Cambridge, Mass.

Popper, Karl (1957) *The Poverty of Historicism*. New York.

————— (1962) *The Open Society and Its Enemies*, 2 vols. New York.

Schutz, Alfred (1967) *The Phenomenology of the Social World*. Evanston.

Searle, John (1969) *Speech Acts*. Cambridge.

Skinner, Quentin (1972*a*) ' "Social Meaning" and the Explanation of Social Action', in P. Laslett et al. (eds.), *Philosophy, Politics and Society*. 4th series, Oxford, pp. 136-57.

————— (1972*b*) 'Motives, Intentions, and the Interpretation of Texts', *New Literary History*, **3**, 393-408.

Weber, Max (1913) 'Ueber einige Kategorien der Verstehenden Soziologie', *Logos*, **4**, 253-94.

————— (1922) *Gesammelte Aufsätze zur Wissenschaftslehre*. Tübingen.

————— (1968) *Economy and Society*. Totowa.

————— (1972) 'George Simmel as Sociologist', *Social Research*, **39**, 155-63.

White, Morton (1965) *Foundations of Historical Knowledge*. New York.

————— (1969) 'Causation and Action', in S. Morgenbesser et al. (eds.), *Philosophy, Science, and Method: Essays in Honor of Ernest Nagel*. New York, pp. 250-59.

Winch, Peter (1958) *The Idea of a Social Science*. London.

INDEX